The All-American
Christmas Cookbook

Family Favorites from Every State

by **GEORGIA ORCUTT**
and **JOHN MARGOLIES**

CHRONICLE BOOKS
SAN FRANCISCO

Library of Congress Cataloging-in-Publication
Data available.

ISBN: 978-0-8118-6144-1

Manufactured in China.

Designed by Margo Mooney

10 9 8 7 6 5 4 3 2 1

Chronicle Books LLC
680 Second Street
San Francisco, California 94107

www.chroniclebooks.com

Dedication

To all the cooks, whatever state you're in, Merry Christmas.

Acknowledgments

We'd like to thank the following people for their generous help in making this book happen: Margo Mooney, for her stellar design talent; Amy Treadwell and Jennifer Sparkman for believing in this idea and watching over it at every stage; our agents, Jim Fitzgerald and Wendy Burton Brouws, for their support and encouragement; Lew Baer, Hal Ottaway, Sherry Sonnett, Joanne Cassullo, and Maria Reidelbach for making images available to us from their collections; and recipe testers Ellen Bradley, Lisa Ceremsak, Karen Chamberlain, Tony Cosentino, Patricia Frawley, Joey Hamill, Stephen Kendall, Andrea Lattuada, Colleen McHugh, Mike Mahar, Jean McLaughlin, Deborah Pidgeon, Rama Raju, Ray Seivwright, Angeliki Spathis, and Michele Young for their enthusiasm and helpful suggestions.

Contents

Here comes Christmas, with all its hustle and bustle, glitter and twitter. It's the time of religious celebration, friends and family, carols and candy canes, parties and presents, Santa and stockings.

In the USA, there's so much to do and so many places to go. Every state offers something special. If you're a superlative sort, you'll want to see the world's largest holiday light display, 300 acres' bright, at the Ogle Bay Resort in West Virginia, or pick up a few things at Bronner's, the world's largest Christmas store, in Frankenmuth, Michigan.

To put that perfect postmark on your Christmas cards, you'll hit the road to mail them from one of the eleven towns named Santa Claus (the one in Indiana boasts a dozen year-round statues of the old boy), the six called Christmas, the three named Noel, or the one called Eggnog. And FYI, the Bethlehem, Connecticut, post office has special Sunday hours and opens daily at 6:30 A.M.

There are so many ways to get into the holiday mood. You can attend Las Noches de las Luminarias in Phoenix; catch the Harbor Stars Christmas fleet parade in Kodiak, Alaska (weather permitting); see the Christmas Car Parade in Bessemer, Arkansas; or enjoy *The Nutcracker* in Boston, Bozeman, Baltimore, and many other cities in between. And you won't want to miss a Christmas ride on the Hocking Valley Scenic Railroad in Ohio; the holiday chocolate sculptures at Ethel M. Chocolates in Las Vegas; the Smoky Mountain Christmas events at Dollywood in Tennessee; or the Chikasha Festival of Light in Oklahoma. You could also stay home and make a Christmas stocking for a new grandchild in Nebraska, or watch the snow fall in New Hampshire.

But always looming, wherever you are, whatever you're doing, is the big question: What will you cook for Christmas this year? Before you make your shopping lists and check them twice, we invite you to come along on a tour of traditions from sea to shining sea and then some. In every state, we'll sample something different and delicious, with easy recipes that are all about feeding friends and family during the holiday season.

Start with the main course. Stuff and roast a goose (South Dakota); fix a turkey with gravy (Minnesota); have baked ham (Delaware); or try a *tourtière* (Rhode Island). Then head down to South Carolina for ambrosia; linger in Louisiana for the perfect baked oyster dressing—it goes with everything; come to Idaho for the world's best mashed potatoes; and then stop by Iowa for classic corn pudding.

CHRISTMAS GREETINGS

Merry Christmas Greetings

HERE'S HOPING THAT
THIS OLD BOY
DID NOT FORGET YOU.
MERRY XMAS

CHRISTMAS GREETINGS

Need some drinks? There's wonderful wassail from Virginia; hot mulled cider from West Virginia; and light, sweet eggnog from Arkansas, still made as it was 200 years ago.

Of course, there are desserts to die for: a chocolate cake from Kentucky that's fit for a king; a succulent plum pudding with hard sauce from Massachusetts; a fabulous fruitcake from Texas (with no green things in it); a cherry torte from Oregon; and a quick peppermint-stick

cake from Utah. And do try not to eat all the maple-walnut fudge from Vermont before the guests arrive. If you need a last-minute gift, forgo the mall and head to the kitchen to make something special: chocolate truffles, peppermint bark, spicy pecans, gingerbread cupcakes.

Santa will arrive soon. He comes to Hawaii in a giant red outrigger canoe and then always manages to cover the entire country in his sleigh. So tie on that apron and go to work. We guarantee you'll have no reason to stop in Humbug, Arizona, this season.

A MERRY CHRISTMAS

Sometime shortly after Thanksgiving, we start thinking about all the things we'll do for Christmas: unearth that tattered old recipe for Grandmother's fruitcake; figure out how to make the *buche de Noël* that looks so perfect in the cookbook photo; bake cookies and make quick breads to give as gifts; and invite the neighbors in for an informal get-together. It all sounds so easy.

But as the holiday draws closer and closer, inevitably the kitchen becomes the focus of frenzied activity. In the midst of plumping raisins and melting chocolate, we're scrambling to feed the family on an unpredictable schedule, baking something for a school project, and often feeling overwhelmed.

Consider these suggestions for making good use of whatever time and space you have available:

Clear away as much kitchen clutter as possible. Be ruthless. Get out a large cardboard box and pack it with all the things you won't use in the next few weeks: the heart-shaped waffle maker, the knickknacks, the herb-garden planter. Stash the box in the basement, or attic, or in a guest-room closet.

Go to work on the refrigerator and get rid of anything that's past its prime. Organize what remains so you have plenty of room to chill wine, cookie dough, or eggnog, and store any perishable food gifts you may receive. And clean out the freezer, too, using up what's on hand to cut down on shopping trips and making room for frozen desserts and holiday leftovers.

Organize a place to work so you have room to roll out dough, arrange racks to let cookies cool, knead bread, and assemble ingredients for a multistep recipe.

Get out the recipes you're planning to make and read them through carefully. Pay special attention to pan sizes, prep and cooking times, and any chilling requirements to avoid surprises. Come up with some menus and make shopping lists.

When people ask if they can help you, say "Yes!" Don't try to do everything yourself. Delegate chores such as chopping nuts, peeling fruit, washing pots and pans.

Alabama

Pecan Divinity

In 1982, the pecan was named the state nut of Alabama, which ranks as the top commercial pecan grower in the United States. This light and airy candy is a popular holiday treat throughout the South, and it makes a fine Christmas gift. It's not difficult to get it right, but seasoned cooks follow a few rules: Don't make it on a rainy day, use a candy thermometer, and be patient, since the final—and very important—beating can take at least eight minutes.

Put the egg whites in a mixing bowl and set aside. Combine the sugar, corn syrup, and water in a large saucepan and stir. Bring to a simmer over medium-low heat and cook until the mixture reaches the soft-ball stage (248°F), about 15 minutes. Remove from the heat. Beat the egg whites with an electric mixer until stiff, glossy peaks form. With the mixer running, pour half of the hot syrup into the whites in a thin stream and continue beating on high speed for 5 more minutes.

May · Xmas
find · you · happy
and · leave · you
happier · still

2	egg whites
3	cups sugar
½	cup corn syrup
½	cup water
1	teaspoon vanilla extract
2	cups broken pecans
36	whole pecans (optional)

New Fashioned Old Fashioned *Recipes*

Mixed Walnut Candies

Velvet Fudge

Divinity

Walnut Mints

Meanwhile, cook the remaining syrup in the pan over medium heat, stirring to keep the syrup from coating the sides of the pan, until it reaches the hard-ball stage (272°F), about 5 minutes. With the mixer running, gradually pour the hot syrup and the vanilla over the egg white mixture. Beat on high speed until the mixture loses its gloss and holds together without sticking to your fingers, about 8 minutes longer. Fold in the pecans.

Using two teaspoons, quickly drop rounded mounds of the mixture onto lightly greased aluminum foil. Press 1 whole pecan, if using, into the top of each piece of candy. Let cool completely and store in a tightly covered container for up to 2 weeks.

Makes 3 dozen pieces

Smoked Salmon and Spinach Strata

Strata, an old-fashioned layered bread dish, is a good choice for a holiday breakfast, since you assemble it one day and bake it the next. When you add Alaska smoked salmon, it's special enough to serve on Christmas morning.

Arrange 6 or 7 slices of the bread in the bottom of a greased 9-by-13-inch baking pan. Brush them lightly with about half of the melted butter. Using your hands, distribute the spinach evenly over the bread. Top the spinach with the smoked salmon. Scatter on the cheese and top with the remaining 6 or 7 slices of bread. Brush the top layer of bread with the remaining melted butter.

Beat the eggs and milk in a large bowl. Slowly pour about half of the egg mixture over the top layer of bread, soaking it thoroughly. Wait for 5 minutes and gradually pour the remaining egg mixture over the top layer of bread. Cover the pan tightly with plastic wrap and refrigerate overnight.

12 to 14	slices white or whole-wheat bread, or a combination, crusts removed
4	tablespoons butter, melted
Two	10-ounce packages frozen chopped spinach, thawed and squeezed dry
4	ounces Alaska smoked salmon
2	cups (8 ounces) shredded Cheddar cheese
10	eggs
2½	cups milk

Heat the oven to 350°F. Remove the strata from the refrigerator and let it sit at room temperature for about 15 minutes. Bake for 45 minutes, or until puffy and lightly browned. Cut into rectangles or squares and serve hot.

Serves 10 to 12

Posole

This spicy corn stew is a traditional Mexican and Native American dish popular throughout the Southwest. Arizona cook Lynn Nusom, who developed this recipe, says it is a "must" on the Christmas Eve or Christmas menu in many Southwestern households. It is also guaranteed to bring good luck if eaten on New Year's Eve. You can make it with chopped cooked chicken or cooked ground chicken, or substitute cooked turkey, pork, beef, or lamb. Serve in large bowls along with your choice of garnishes: red chile sauce, chopped onion, sliced radishes, sliced cabbage, or lime wedges.

Combine all the ingredients in a large pot and cook over low heat for 1 hour or until all the flavors are blended. Or, cook in a slow cooker for 4 hours on high or 8 hours on low.

Serves 4 to 6 as a main course

Greetings from SANTA CLAUS, ARIZONA
CHRISTMAS TREE INN
★ ★
OLIVES — CELERY — ICEBERG
★
ESKIMO FRUIT COCKTAIL
or
NORTH SEA SHRIMP COCKTAIL
★
POINSETTIA TOMATO SOUP
or
REINDEER and CHICKEN SOUP
★
CHOICE of
CHICKEN A LA SNOW WHITE
MARY'S LITTLE LAMB CHOPS
FILET MIGNON A LA SANTA CLAUS
★
SNOW SHERBET
★
EVERGREEN SALAD
or
NORTH POLE SALAD
★
CHOICE of
MORNING GLORY ICE CREAM
KRISKRINGLE RUM PIE
FAIRYLAND PIE
STARDUST CAKE
★
DWARF COFFEE
NUTS — MINTS

OB-H2427

4	cups chopped cooked chicken, or 2 pounds ground chicken, cooked
Two	15-ounce cans white hominy, drained
6	cups chicken broth
1	onion, chopped
½	cup chopped green chiles or jalapeños
2	cloves garlic, minced
1	teaspoon dried oregano
1	teaspoon ground black pepper
1	tablespoon red chile powder
1	teaspoon ground cumin
	Juice of 1 lime

Arizona Christmas Foods

Circular 266

Agricultural Extension Service, University of Arizona, Tucson

Nicholas Peay's Eggnog

Eggnog has been made by many generations of the Peay and Worthen families, who have always believed that the real thing contains only eggs, sugar, and spirits—no dairy. Nicholas Peay, who served in the War of 1812 and the Indian Wars, came to Little Rock in the territorial period and in 1826 opened one of the city's first hotels. Today, his great-great-great-grandson, Bill Worthen, director of the Historic Arkansas Museum, makes two batches of eggnog for the staff Christmas party each year. The treasured recipe usually wins the museum's mid-December Nog-Off, a competition for the best eggnog in town.

1	dozen eggs, separated
1	cup sugar
1	cup bourbon

Beat the yolks with an electric mixer on medium speed until they are yellow and creamy, about 4 minutes. While the mixer is running, beat the whites with an egg beater until stiff, glossy peaks form. Set aside. Gradually add the sugar to the yolks and continue to beat 1 minute longer, or until the mixture is very light. Add the liquor slowly, beating constantly 1 minute more. Fold in the beaten whites and serve at once in punch cups or small mugs.

Serves 12 to 14

Note: There is some concern in food circles that raw eggs can carry the risk of salmonella. Bill Worthen remains steadfast in his resolve to continue making this special eggnog for family

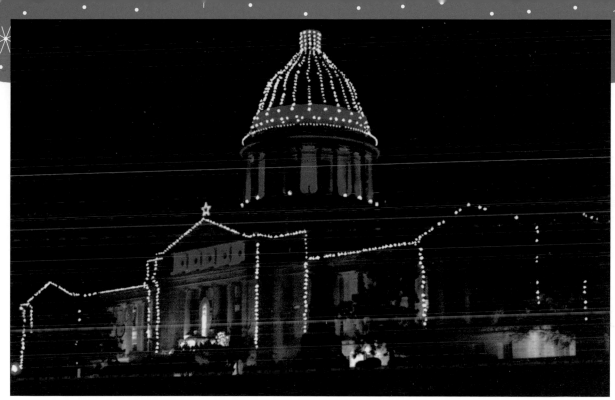

and friends the way it's been done for almost 200 years. "No one has suffered yet," he explains, "except in the usual holiday-appropriate ways!"

For readers who remain skittish, the American Egg Board recommends cooked eggnog: In a large saucepan, beat together 6 eggs, ¼ cup sugar, and ¼ teaspoon salt. Add 2 cups skim or 1 percent milk and cook over low heat, stirring constantly, until the mixture reaches 160°F, just thick enough to coat a metal spoon with a thin film. Remove from the heat; add 2 more cups milk and 1 teaspoon vanilla extract. Cover and refrigerate until thoroughly chilled, several hours or overnight. Pour into a pitcher and serve immediately, garnished with ground nutmeg, brandy or liqueur, or chocolate curls.

Christmas Joys

CALIFORNIA'S WINTER IS GOOD ENOUGH FOR ME

Fuyu Persimmon and Radicchio Salad

For more than 50 years, California has led the country in agricultural production. It has also inspired innovative thinking and awareness of how food is grown and made, and how it is presented at the table. The Center for Urban Education about Sustainable Agriculture (CUESA), organized in San Francisco in 1994, manages the Ferry Plaza Farmers' Market, which connects urban dwellers with local farmers who practice sustainable agriculture. CUESA vice president Peggy Knickerbocker, journalist and author of *Simple Soirées* and the *Ferry Plaza Farmers' Market Cookbook,* created this salad to deliver a dash of California style to the Christmas table. The colors are beautiful—red, orange, green, and white. The pomegranate seeds provide a good crunch, and the feta a nice saltiness against the sweet persimmon.

2	tablespoons apple cider balsamic vinegar, or 2 tablespoons red wine vinegar plus a few drops of good balsamic vinegar
1	shallot, minced
	Sea salt and freshly ground pepper
3	Fuyu persimmons, peeled and thinly sliced crosswise
1	head radicchio, cored and thinly sliced
2	cups small arugula leaves
¼	cup crumbled feta cheese
⅓	cup extra-virgin olive oil
	Handful of pomegranate seeds

WITH BEST WISHES FOR A MERRY CHRISTMAS AND A HAPPY NEW YEAR FROM CALIFORNIA

A midwinter scene

Pour the vinegar into a small bowl, add the shallot, and season with salt and pepper to taste. Set aside. Combine the persimmons, radicchio, arugula, and about two-thirds of the feta in a salad bowl. Whisk the olive oil into the vinegar mixture. Toss the salad with the dressing. Divide among 4 to 6 salad plates and scatter a bit of the remaining feta and pomegranate seeds over the top of each serving.

Serves 4 to 6 as a first course

P-10 THE CHRISTMAS TREE STREET, SANTA ROSA AVENUE, ALTADENA, CALIFORNIA

Caramelized Lamb Roast with Apricot and Cranberry Stuffing

When American chefs think of lamb, many think of Colorado lamb, known for its sweet taste and large, juicy cuts. It's no coincidence that Vail hosts the annual Colorado Lamb Cook-Off, where professional cooks put this local favorite through its paces. Try this dish for a holiday dinner and serve with mashed potatoes, corn pudding, and cranberry sauce. Reheat leftovers in barbecue sauce and enjoy in hearty sandwiches.

1	Colorado lamb leg, 5 to 6 pounds, butterflied
	Salt and freshly ground pepper
⅔	cup dried apricots, snipped into ¼-inch pieces
⅔	cup dried cranberries
1	tablespoon olive oil
¼	cup finely chopped red onion
2	tablespoons chopped fresh rosemary
½	teaspoon salt
¼	teaspoon freshly ground black pepper
⅓	cup orange juice
2	teaspoons ground cinnamon
½	cup dark corn syrup

Heat the oven to 500°F. Place the lamb flat on a cutting board and trim off all visible fat. Using a meat mallet, flatten the lamb so it is of even thickness and about 2 inches thick. Season with salt and pepper. Set aside.

Combine the apricots and cranberries in a small bowl and set aside. Heat the oil in a small skillet over medium-high heat. Add the onion, rosemary, ½ teaspoon salt, and ¼ teaspoon pepper and sauté for 3 to 4 minutes, or until the onion is soft and the mixture is fragrant. Add the orange juice and cinnamon and bring to a boil. Pour the mixture over the apricots and cranberries and let stand for 15 minutes.

Meanwhile, cut 16 lengths of kitchen twine, each about 20 inches long. Cut the meat in half, making two rectangles. Divide the filling between the two pieces of meat and spread it as evenly as possible

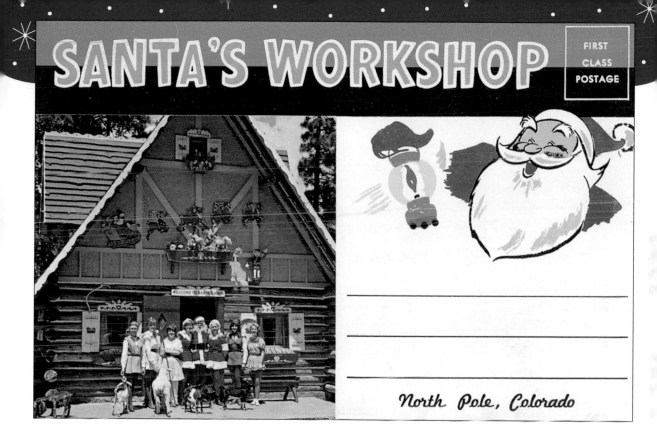

SANTA'S WORKSHOP

North Pole, Colorado

over each piece. Starting at the smallest end, roll the meat up as tightly as possible. Place it, seam side down, on the cutting board and tightly tie twine around it at 1-inch intervals. Repeat with the second piece of meat to form 2 roasts. Place the meat on a rack in a large roasting pan.

Place the meat in the oven and immediately reduce the temperature to 325°F. Roast for 15 minutes. Baste the meat with the corn syrup

and roast, basting with the remaining syrup every 15 minutes, for a total of 50 to 60 minutes, or until an instant-read thermometer inserted in the center of a roast registers 145°F for medium-rare, 160°F for medium. Remove from the oven, loosely tent with aluminum foil, and let sit for 10 minutes. Snip off the twine and slice the meat into ½-inch-thick pieces. Serve warm or at room temperature.

Serves 10 to 12

The Best-Ever Butter Cookies

In 1958, the year her first child was born, Alice Lehr of Branford asked her husband, Loren, to invite a few friends from work to stop by for cookies and eggnog. From this humble gathering Alice's famous cookie party was launched. Neighbors say it's the first date they write on their calendars for the new year. Starting weeks in advance, Alice bakes and freezes more than 2,000 cookies from refrigerator dough, including these butter cookies. Each year cookie-party guests put a quarter in a jar and try to guess the exact number. The winner gets the money and, along with everyone who attends, goes home with a selection of cookies.

5	cups all-purpose flour
2	teaspoons baking powder
½	teaspoon salt
2	cups (4 sticks) butter, softened
1½	cups sugar
2	eggs
1	teaspoon vanilla extract

Quick Icing

2	tablespoons butter
3	cups confectioners' sugar, sifted
3 to 4	tablespoons milk
⅛	teaspoon vanilla extract

Combine the flour, baking powder, and salt in a large bowl. Stir with a whisk to blend. Set aside. Cream the butter and sugar in a mixing bowl with an electric mixer. Beat in the eggs and vanilla. Gradually add the flour mixture to the butter mixture, about 1 cup at a time, beating well after each addition. Cover the dough with plastic wrap and refrigerate overnight.

Heat the oven to 375°F. Roll out one-quarter of the dough to a ⅛-inch thickness on a lightly floured board. (Keep the remaining dough refrigerated as you work.) Cut the dough into desired shapes with floured cookie cutters. Place the cookies 1 inch apart on ungreased baking sheets and bake until lightly browned, 6 to 8 minutes. Let cool for a few minutes on the baking sheet, then transfer to a wire rack to cool completely.

To make the icing: Melt the butter over low heat in a medium saucepan. Remove from the heat. Stir in the sugar and then gradually stir in the milk until the icing reaches the desired consistency. Stir in the vanilla. Add a drop of food coloring if you wish, and thin the icing if necessary by adding just a drop or two more of milk. Frost the cookies while the icing is still soft.

Makes 2 to 3 dozen

Baked Ham with Madeira Sauce and Browned Potatoes

Horticulturist and collector Henry Francis du Pont, who turned his magnificent country estate into the Winterthur Museum in 1951, was born on the property in 1880 and died there in 1969. Christmas at Winterthur has always been a special time. Today, approximately 20,000 visitors stop by for the Yuletide at Winterthur tour, when the rooms are beautifully decorated and the dining room table set as if for an elaborate meal. This recipe, from the Winterthur archives, makes a festive holiday dish that was a favorite of the du Pont family.

1	uncooked country ham, 6 to 7 pounds
3	quarts beef broth
2	onions, thinly sliced
3	shallots, thinly sliced
4	carrots, peeled and grated
2	cups Madeira wine
1	clove garlic, crushed
1¼	cups water, plus 2 tablespoons
8	potatoes, peeled and halved
1	tablespoon flour
	Freshly ground pepper
1	tablespoon butter

Put the ham in a large stainless-steel pot and soak it for 24 hours in cold water to remove excess salt. Change the water at least 3 times during the soaking period. Drain. Add the broth, cover the pot, and bring to a boil over medium-high heat. Reduce the heat to medium-low and simmer gently for 1½ hours. Remove the ham from the heat and let it sit for several hours to cool in the broth. Drain the ham and set it on a large cutting board. Remove the rind and trim off any excess fat. Reserve the fat.

Heat the oven to 450°F. Put several pieces of reserved ham fat into a large casserole dish and render over medium-low heat. Add the onions, shallots, and carrots and cook for 5 minutes, or until soft. Add the Madeira, garlic, and the 1¼ cups of water. Put the ham on top of the vegetables and arrange the potatoes around the edges. Place the dish in the oven and immediately reduce the heat to 350°F. Bake for 2 hours, basting the ham with pan juices and turning it every 30 minutes so it will brown evenly. When the bone can be pulled out but still offers some resistance, the ham is done.

Arrange the ham and potatoes on a platter and cover them with aluminum foil to keep warm. Strain the pan drippings into a saucepan set over medium heat. Dissolve the flour in the 2 tablespoons water and whisk it into the sauce to thicken it. Season with pepper to taste. Remove the sauce from the heat, stir in the butter, and beat until smooth. Serve the sauce in a gravy boat, along with the ham and potatoes.

Serves 12

Note: This recipe calls for a true country ham, cured without the water and chemical injections typical of a supermarket ham. It's very salty and must be soaked before cooking. Leftovers taste best sliced paper thin and served cold or at room temperature. Look online for sources. Calhoun's Country Hams supplies many of America's top restaurants.

ALWAYS A CHAIR FOR YOU

A Merry Christmas

Christmas Flan

Noche buena, the traditional Latino Christmas Eve celebration, is an especially festive time in Miami. Families of Puerto Rican, Mexican, and Cuban descent gather to enjoy special dishes from their native regions. Some will roast a whole pig, and most will enjoy a flan for dessert. Allow at least 2 hours for the flan to chill and firm before serving.

Arrange six 7-ounce ramekins in a shallow baking dish and set aside.

To make the caramel: Combine the orange juice and sugar in a medium saucepan, stir to blend, and bring to a boil over medium heat. Simmer without stirring for about 5 minutes, or until the bubbling syrup turns a light caramel color. Remove the pan from the heat and very carefully divide the caramel evenly among the ramekins. Let the caramel harden, about 10 minutes.

To make the custard: Put a teakettle full of water on to boil. Combine all the ingredients in a mixing bowl and blend with a whisk until smooth. Distribute evenly among the ramekins. Pour enough boiling water into the baking dish to come about halfway up the sides of the ramekins.

Caramel
¼   cup orange juice
1½   cups sugar

Custard
One   14-ounce can sweetened condensed milk
¾   cup milk
6   eggs
2   teaspoons vanilla extract

Heat the oven to 350°F. Bake for 30 to 40 minutes, or until a knife inserted in the center comes out clean and the custards don't jiggle. Remove the ramekins from the oven, take them out of the water bath, and set them on a wire rack to cool for about 30 minutes. Arrange them on a tray, cover loosely with a sheet of aluminum foil, and refrigerate overnight.

To serve, run a knife along the inside edge of a ramekin, invert a dessert plate over the ramekin, then, holding onto the ramekin with one hand, invert again and remove the ramekin.

Serves 6

Variation: To dress up the flan, peel and chop 3 oranges, combine with several tablespoons of Cointreau and 2 tablespoons confectioners' sugar in a bowl, and let sit at room temperature while the flans cool. Spoon the fruit to the side of each flan before serving.

HOLSUM BAKERY 1955 HOLIDAY DISPLAY
SOUTH MIAMI ON SUNSET ROAD – EAST OF HWY 1 – DECEMBER 10th THRU JANUARY 2ND

Cranberry-Pecan Chutney

Between 1910 and 1925, thousands of acres of pecan trees were planted in Georgia, and since the 1950s the state has been the nation's top producer. Georgia pecans grow large and sweet. They're easy to enjoy all by themselves, and they make a fine addition to holiday cookies, candies, and snacks. Georgia cook Anne Byrn was inspired to use them in this tangy, chunky, and colorful relish that is especially appealing when served in a glass bowl. Try this instead of the traditional cranberry sauce as an accompaniment to roast turkey, goose, beef, or ham.

1	pound fresh or frozen cranberries
2	cinnamon sticks
½	teaspoon ground allspice
⅛	teaspoon ground cloves
½	teaspoon salt
1	cup water
1	large unpeeled apple, cored and diced
1	cup golden raisins or chopped dried apricots
4	thin lemon slices, seeded and cut into quarters
1½	cups sugar
1	cup chopped celery
½	cup chopped sweet onion
½	cup chopped pecans

Combine the cranberries, cinnamon, allspice, cloves, salt, and water in a large saucepan. Stir to combine. Bring to a boil over high heat, then reduce the heat to medium-low and simmer until the berries begin to pop, about 10 minutes. Remove the pan from the heat and stir in the apple, raisins, lemon slices, sugar, celery, and onion. Cook over medium heat, stirring several

HARVEY'S PECAN STATION AND TRAILER COURT

HARVEYS PECAN STATION

16 MILES SOUTH OF ATLANTA ON U. S. HIGHWAY 41 AND 19

Rich's Department Store, Atlanta, Georgia

times, for 5 minutes. Cover, reduce the heat to medium-low, and simmer for 30 minutes. Uncover and cook 15 minutes longer, or until thick. Remove from the heat and let cool for 30 minutes. Remove the cinnamon sticks. Stir in the pecans, transfer to one or several containers with tight-fitting lids, and refrigerate.

Makes about 4 cups

Note: This sauce will keep for about a week in the refrigerator. If you want to give it a longer shelf life, spoon it into 4 sterilized pint jars and process in a hot-water bath for 10 minutes. Store in a cool, dark place for up to 3 months.

Pineapple-Macadamia Nut Loaf Cake with Pineapple Sauce

Christmas comes to Hawaii in its own special way: Santa arrives in a magical bright-red outrigger canoe, "Silent Night" is played on ukuleles, Christmas dinner may include a pig roasted at a backyard lu'au, and you'll hear "Mele Kalikimaka" instead of "Merry Christmas." This moist holiday dessert, which makes a fine substitute for pound cake or can be served as a sweet bread, uses two of the foods often associated with the Aloha State. Hawaii led the world in pineapple production into the early 1960s and was the world's largest producer of macadamia nuts until the late 1990s. The recipe is easy to assemble on a countertop when there's considerable activity in the kitchen. Put it in the oven just as you sit down for dinner and serve it warm, topped with warm sauce.

3	cups all-purpose flour
1	tablespoon baking powder
4	eggs
1	cup sugar
½	cup canola oil
¾	cup pineapple juice (see Note)
½	cup canned crushed pineapple
¾	cup chopped macadamia nuts

Pineapple Sauce

¼	cup sugar
1¼	cups pineapple juice
1	tablespoon cornstarch
1	tablespoon butter
¼	teaspoon freshly grated nutmeg
1½	cups canned crushed pineapple

Heat the oven to 350°F. Lightly grease a 9-by-5-inch loaf pan and line the bottom and sides with waxed paper. Trim any paper that hangs over the edges. Combine the flour and baking powder in a bowl and blend with a whisk until smooth. Combine the eggs, sugar, oil, and pineapple juice in a second bowl and stir until well blended. Add the dry ingredients and stir just until evenly moistened. Fold in the pineapple and macadamia nuts. Scrape the batter into the prepared pan. Place the loaf pan on a baking sheet (a bit of juice may spill over in the oven) and bake for 50 to 60 minutes, or until the cake is puffy and brown and a toothpick inserted in the center comes out clean. Let cool on a wire rack for 30 minutes.

To make the sauce: Combine the sugar and pineapple juice in a medium saucepan and cook over medium-high heat until the mixture just begins to boil. Add the cornstarch, reduce the heat to medium, and whisk until smooth. Continue cooking for 5 minutes, or until the sauce thickens. Stir in the butter and nutmeg and cook for 1 minute longer. Add the pineapple and cook until heated through.

Unmold the cake, cut it into slices, and serve topped with pineapple sauce.

Note: Buy two 20-ounce cans of crushed pineapple. Drain them in a strainer over a bowl, pressing gently on the pineapple to coax out as much juice as possible.

Serves 8 to 10

Baked Mashed Potatoes

Since the 1860s, Idaho has been known for its potatoes, which must be grown in the state to have the word *Idaho* printed on the bag. At Christmastime, mashed potatoes are a must-have item, but they get cold in a heartbeat, especially during the buzz of holiday dinners when it takes a while to get everyone settled at the table. Here's an easy way to serve hot mashed potatoes at a party or bring them all set to go when you're invited elsewhere. Assemble and refrigerate this dish up to a day ahead of time. Let the dish sit at room temperature for 30 minutes, and then bake it. These potatoes go with everything—roast turkey, goose, ham, or roast beef—and they hold up beautifully on a buffet table.

Put the potatoes in a large pot of salted water, bring to a boil, and cook for about 20 minutes, or until they can be easily pierced with a fork. Drain and immediately mash or, for the very best consistency, press them through a ricer. Add the butter and milk and mix well.

Heat the oven to 350°F. Lightly grease an 8-cup casserole. Combine the egg, sour cream, and cottage cheese in a mixing bowl and beat at medium speed with an electric mixer until smooth. Add the chives and potatoes and beat on low speed until evenly mixed. Spoon the potatoes into the prepared dish and top with the shredded cheese. Bake for 30 minutes, or until the edges are lightly browned. Serve hot.

Serves 10 to 12

8 to 10	Idaho potatoes, peeled and cut into chunks
4	tablespoons butter, cut into bits
½	cup milk
1	egg
1	cup sour cream
1	cup small-curd cottage cheese
2	tablespoons chopped fresh chives, or 4 diced scallions (white part only)
½	cup (2 ounces) shredded Cheddar cheese

We Love Good Santa, and We Know
His Boundless Generosity —
It's up to US, sometimes, to Show
Some Christmas Reciprocity —

DERE SANTY
CLAWS
MERRY XMAS
HELP YURESELF
AND DONT FERGIT
YOUR FREND

HIGH BRIDGE
LAWYERS CANYON, IDAHO, 296 FT.
No. 5.

GREETINGS
FROM IDAHO

Hail
Happy
Christmas Tide!

Seafood Lasagna

Before World War I, a stream of Italian immigrants settled in Chicago and its suburbs. On Christmas Eve in cities and towns throughout Illinois, third- and fourth-generation Italian Americans sit down to the traditional feast that includes numerous seafood dishes. Here's a special recipe created by Italian cooking diva Deborah Mele. It combines pasta with several kinds of seafood and can be served hot or at room temperature.

To make the béchamel: Melt the butter in a heavy saucepan over low heat. Add the flour and stir for a minute or two until the flour just begins to take on some color. Gradually add the milk, whisking constantly to prevent lumps from forming. Simmer, stirring frequently, until the sauce begins to thicken. Season with the salt, white pepper, and nutmeg. Pour the sauce into a bowl, cover with a sheet of buttered plastic wrap to prevent a skin from forming on top, and set aside.

To make the spinach: Coarsely chop the spinach and microwave until wilted. Add the oil and garlic, season with salt and pepper to taste, and toss to blend. Set aside.

To make the seafood: Coarsely chop the shrimp and scallops. Cut the salmon into 1-inch pieces. Melt 1 tablespoon of the butter with 1 tablespoon of the oil in a large, heavy skillet over medium heat. Add the shrimp, season with salt and pepper to taste, and cook just until pink, about 3 minutes. Remove from the pan. In the same pan, melt the remaining 1 tablespoon butter with the remaining 1 tablespoon oil and cook the scallops just until opaque, about 3 minutes. Remove from the pan and cook the salmon in the remaining pan juices just until opaque, about 4 minutes. Set aside.

To assemble the lasagna: Cook the noodles until al dente, about 8 minutes for dried noodles

Béchamel

4	tablespoons butter
¼	cup all-purpose flour
2	cups milk
	Pinch of salt, ground white pepper, and ground nutmeg

Spinach

1	pound spinach, washed and dried
1	tablespoon olive oil
1	clove garlic, finely chopped
	Salt and freshly ground pepper

Seafood

1	pound shrimp, shelled and deveined
1	pound sea scallops
One	6-ounce salmon steak or fillet, pin bones and skin removed
2	tablespoons butter
2	tablespoons olive oil
	Salt and freshly ground black pepper
1	pound lasagna noodles, preferably homemade
4	cups tomato sauce
½	cup grated romano cheese
1	cup shredded mozzarella or fontina cheese

and about 4 minutes for fresh. Run under cold water, and drain. Heat the oven to 350°F. Spread about ½ cup tomato sauce along the bottom of a 9-by-13-inch baking pan. Arrange a layer of lasagna noodles on top of the tomato sauce, and spread the noodles with half of the béchamel. Dot with the shrimp and half of the salmon. Add another layer of noodles, then half of the remaining tomato sauce, half of the spinach, and the romano cheese. Add another layer of noodles, the remaining béchamel, the rest of the salmon, and the scallops. Add the remaining noodles, the rest of the tomato sauce, and the remaining spinach. Top with the mozzarella. Bake for 40 to 45 minutes, or until bubbly and golden brown. Let sit for 10 minutes before serving.

Serves 8 to 10

Lebkuchen

Two weeks before Christmas, the Conner Prairie Museum in Indianapolis hosts a festival of gingerbread houses, where a stunning variety of seasonal architecture and gingerbread in many forms is celebrated—and eaten. Several versions of this light-colored, spicy German Christmas cookie came to Indiana as early as 1814 with religious leader George Rapp and his followers, who built the town of New Harmony on the Wabash River. This recipe was created by the late Betty Kuebler-McGlothlin of Brown County, a longtime member of the Indiana German Heritage Society.

4½	cups all-purpose flour
½	teaspoon baking soda
½	teaspoon salt
1	teaspoon ground cinnamon
1	teaspoon ground cloves
2	teaspoons ground ginger (optional)
½	teaspoon ground allspice
4	eggs
1	cup granulated sugar
1	cup firmly packed brown sugar
⅔	cup honey
1½	cups slivered almonds
1	cup dried fruit such as raisins and cherries, or mixed diced candied fruit

Icing

2½	cups confectioners' sugar, sifted
6	tablespoons evaporated milk
	Colored sugar sprinkles (optional)

Greetings from SANTA CLAUS INDIANA

© CURT TEICH & CO., INC.

Visit
SANTA CLAUS
LAND
SANTA CLAUS
IND.

*Christmas
Room*

fine foods from famous

SANTA CLAUS LAND

SANTA CLAUS, INDIANA

Heat the oven to 350°F. Grease two baking sheets, one 11 by 17 inches, the other 9 by 13 inches. Combine the flour, baking soda, salt, cinnamon, cloves, ginger, if using, and allspice in a large bowl and blend with a whisk. Set aside. Beat the eggs in a bowl with an electric mixer until light. Add the sugars and honey and beat until smooth. With the mixer on low speed, gradually add in the flour mixture, beating just until the dough is smooth. Add the almonds and fruit and beat just until they are mixed in. Turn about two-thirds of the dough out onto the larger baking sheet, one-third onto the smaller. Dip your hands in flour and spread the dough evenly, pressing it toward the perimeter of the pans, until it forms an even layer.

Bake for 15 minutes, or until lightly browned and the edges start to pull away from the sides of the pans. (If both baking sheets won't fit on one rack in your oven, use two racks and switch their positions after 8 minutes.) Let cool in the pans for about 10 minutes before icing.

To make the icing: Combine the confectioners' sugar and evaporated milk in a small bowl and stir until smooth. Brush a thin layer onto the cookies while they are still slightly warm. Immediately sprinkle the cookies with sugar sprinkles, if using. Let cool completely and cut into pieces about 2½ inches square. Transfer to an airtight container, using waxed paper to separate the layers.

Makes about 4½ dozen

Variation: For a thicker cookie, use just one large baking sheet and bake for about 20 minutes.

Corn Pudding

Iowa is the country's number-one corn producer, and a bountiful source of recipes for this classic side dish. Bethia Waterman of Davenport, who sent friends a photo of herself biking through the Iowa cornfields in last year's Christmas card, takes her mother Ruth's recipe and enhances it by adding cheese and a can of whole-kernel corn. Sometimes she also adds chiles for zip. You can mix this pudding up to one day ahead and bake it along with the turkey or ham. Or, bake it in advance and reheat in the microwave until piping hot.

Heat the oven to 350°F. Lightly grease an 8-cup casserole dish. Combine the eggs and milk in a large bowl and blend with a whisk until smooth. Whisk in the sugar, cornstarch, and salt and let the mixture sit for several minutes until the cornstarch dissolves. Stir in the corn and cheese. Pour into the prepared dish and dot with the butter.

Bake for 1 hour, stirring once after 20 minutes, or until the top is browned and the center is set. Let sit for 10 minutes before serving.

Serves 6 to 8 as a side dish

A MERRY CHRISTMAS

Good Christmas wishes without number,
My heart goes with my thought.
And long may this happiness endure,
In the spirit of Christmas brought.

2	eggs
1	cup milk
2	tablespoons sugar
2	tablespoons cornstarch
½	teaspoon salt
One	14¾-ounce can creamed corn
One	15¼-ounce can unsweetened whole-kernel corn
½	cup (2 ounces) shredded Cheddar cheese
2	tablespoons butter, cut into bits

A MERRY CHRISTMAS

GREETINGS FROM KEOKUK, IOWA.

R. F. ROLLING, PUB.

LOWER LOCK, GOVERNMENT CANAL, KEOKUK, IOWA.

A MERRY CHRISTMAS

GREETINGS FROM KEOKUK, IOWA.

R. F. ROLLING, PUBL.

MISSISSIPPI RIVER POWER CO'S DAM AT KEOKUK, IOWA.

41

Coffee Cake for a Crowd

Kansas has a number of nicknames, among them the Sunflower State and the Cyclone State. But perhaps the most fitting is the Wheat State, a reminder that it is the nation's top wheat producer. By one estimate, a year's average crop would fill train cars stretching east from the state's western border all the way to the Atlantic Ocean. Not surprisingly, home baking is promoted throughout the state. Make this moist and fragrant coffee cake, which contains no eggs and very little fat per serving, when you have a houseful of holiday guests or are planning a Christmas coffee get-together. It easily serves 20 people, and keeps well for a week, tightly covered.

2	cups low-fat milk
2	tablespoons cider vinegar
3	cups all-purpose flour
1	cup granulated sugar
1	cup packed brown sugar
2	teaspoons ground cinnamon
½	teaspoon cloves
½	teaspoon salt
½	cup vegetable shortening (preferably nonhydrogenated)
¾	cup diced dates
2	teaspoons baking soda
1	tablespoon butter or vegetable shortening
¼	cup chopped walnuts or pecans
¼	cup shredded sweetened coconut
1	teaspoon grated orange zest

Heat the oven to 350°F. Grease and flour a 9-by-13-inch baking pan; knock out the excess flour. Combine the milk and vinegar in a small bowl and set aside.

Combine the flour, sugars, cinnamon, cloves, and salt in a large bowl and stir with a whisk to blend. Using a pastry cutter or your fingertips, mix the shortening into the dry ingredients until crumbly. Reserve ¼ cup of the mixture. Add the dates to the remaining dry ingredients and toss gently. Stir the baking soda into the milk mixture and add to the dry ingredients, stirring just until evenly moistened. Pour the batter into the prepared pan.

In a food processor, combine the reserved ¼ cup flour mixture, the butter, nuts, coconut, and zest. Process just until blended. Sprinkle the topping evenly over the batter. (At this point, the coffee cake can be covered and refrigerated for 24 hours.) Bake for 45 minutes, or until a toothpick inserted in the center comes out clean. Let cool on a wire rack. Serve warm or at room temperature.

Variations: Use diced dried apricots, diced prunes, raisins, currants, or other dried fruit in place of the dates. If using raisins, soak them for 10 minutes in cold water to plump them, then drain before adding to the batter.

Serves 20

Chocolate Celebration Cake

Kentucky-born chef David Larson was apprentice to a number of top cooking pros before opening his acclaimed restaurant, the Pampered Chef, in Lexington. He's also the chef-in-residence at Labrot and Graham Distillery in Versailles, where bourbon is still made in copper pot stills. Using the company's smooth Woodford Reserve bourbon, David created this sinfully rich and wonderful cake, which promises to deliver a fabulous finale to a no-holds-barred Christmas dinner. Make it up to one week in advance and store, covered, in the refrigerator.

8	ounces semisweet chocolate, coarsely chopped
4	ounces bittersweet chocolate, coarsely chopped
1½	cups (3 sticks) unsalted butter at room temperature
1¼	cups sugar
3	tablespoons bourbon
10	eggs, separated
2	cups ground pecans
	Confectioners' sugar for dusting

Christmas Yuletide Lighting of City Park

Heat the oven to 350°F. Grease the bottom and sides of a 10-inch springform pan. Line the bottom of the pan with a round of parchment paper; grease the paper. Combine the two chocolates in a double boiler and melt over barely simmering water, stirring frequently.

Combine the butter and sugar in a mixing bowl and beat with an electric mixer until light, scraping the bowl several times. Beat in the bourbon. Add the egg yolks, one at a time, beating well after each addition. Continue beating until the mixture is very smooth. Beat the egg whites in a separate bowl until stiff, glossy peaks form. Fold the egg whites into the egg yolk mixture alternately with the chocolate and pecans. Spoon the batter into the prepared pan. Bake for 50 to 55 minutes, or until the center is set. Let cool in the pan on a wire rack for 1 hour. Remove the sides of the pan. Dust with confectioners' sugar and cut into slices.

Serves 8 to 10

Louisiana

Corn Bread-Oyster Dressing

As the nation's top producer, Louisiana markets as many as 750 million oysters annually, many enjoyed raw on the half shell by visitors to New Orleans. Although the hurricanes of 2005 significantly affected the oyster industry throughout the Gulf of Mexico, recovery is under way. Oysters are often used at Christmastime in this Louisiana classic, which is baked and served as a side dish with ham, turkey, seafood, or beef. Carolyn Griffen of Shreveport shares her family recipe, but recalls that her mother never measured, just put the dressing together by taste. The trick, she says, is to add just enough chicken broth so the dressing isn't too dry, but not so much that it won't be firm when serving. For the best flavor, mix the dressing one day ahead and refrigerate, tightly covered, until ready to bake.

Two	8½-ounce packages corn bread mix, baked, or one 9-by-13-inch pan of your favorite recipe
¾ to 1	loaf sliced white bread
2	pints shucked oysters with their liquor
½	cup (1 stick) butter
2	onions, chopped
1	green bell pepper, seeded and chopped
1 to 2	bunches scallions (white parts only), chopped
10	stalks celery, chopped
4	eggs, beaten
¼	cup chopped fresh flat-leaf parsley
2	teaspoons poultry seasoning or to taste
	Salt and freshly ground pepper
4 to 5	cups chicken broth

Combine the mixes, if using, and prepare according to the package directions. Bake in a 9-by-13-inch pan for 15 minutes, or until lightly browned on top. Set aside to cool.

Heat the oven to 275°F. Lightly grease a 3 quart baking dish. Arrange the slices of white bread on a baking sheet and bake for about 20 minutes, or until brown and dry. Pulse the toasted bread slices in batches in a food processor to make crumbs. Transfer to a large bowl. Crumble the corn bread into the bowl and toss gently with the bread crumbs.

Put the oysters and their liquor in a small saucepan and simmer over medium-low heat for about 5 minutes, or just until the edges curl. Remove the oysters, saving the liquor, and cut in half; if they are very large, cut them in quarters. Return the oysters to the pan and set aside.

Melt the butter in a large skillet over medium-low heat. Add the onions, bell pepper, scallions, and celery and sauté for about 8 minutes, stirring occasionally, until the vegetables are very soft. Add the sautéed vegetables to the bread crumbs and toss. Add the eggs to the bread along with

the parsley, poultry seasoning, and salt and pepper to taste. Add the oysters and their liquor and enough chicken broth to evenly moisten the bread crumbs. Toss gently to mix.

Transfer the mixture to the prepared baking dish and bake for about 1 hour, or until the top is nicely browned and the center is firm. Serve hot or at room temperature.

Serves 8 to 10 as a side dish

Variations: For a festive touch, use 1 small red bell pepper and 1 green.

Omit the corn bread and use 8 cups toasted French bread cubes.

Simmer several chicken livers and gizzards for 30 minutes in enough water to cover, and use some of that broth for the dressing. Add the chopped giblets to the dressing along with the oysters.

Prepare the dressing ahead of time without the oysters and freeze it. Let it thaw in the refrigerator for 24 hours. Add the oysters with their liquor and bake.

Lobster Chowder

Lobster, the state food of Maine, offers all sorts of possibilities for a fabulous Christmastime meal: Forgo the turkey or ham and simply steam or boil one lobster per person; turn to the classic lobster Newburg, a blend of lobster, eggs, and cream; or make this very special chowder, created by New England chef Jasper White, who promises it will give you a Boothbay Harbor vacation in a bowl. In the winter, lobsters can be expensive, so he recommends allowing half a small lobster per person. Set aside time to make this chowder in advance, then gently reheat it for an instant Christmas Eve feast or a sublime first course on Christmas Day.

PECK'S AND ALL MAINE SEND YOU A WARM CHRISTMAS GREETING!

SANTA CLAUS
Cordially Invites You
To Join Our
CHRISTMAS CLUB
NORWAY
SAVINGS BANK
NORWAY, MAINE

3	live hard-shell lobsters (up to 1¼ pounds each)

Lobster Stock

	Reserved lobster carcasses and shells, above
8	cups water
1	cup dry white wine
1	cup chopped fresh or canned tomatoes with their juice
2	onions, thinly sliced
2	stalks celery, thinly sliced
2	small carrots, thinly sliced
4	cloves garlic, crushed
4	sprigs fresh thyme
2	dried bay leaves
¼	teaspoon fennel seeds
1	teaspoon black peppercorns
	Kosher or sea salt

One	4-ounce slab (unsliced) bacon, rind removed, cut into ⅓-inch dice
4	tablespoons unsalted butter
1	large onion, cut into ¾-inch dice
	Leaves from 2 to 3 sprigs fresh thyme, chopped (about 1 teaspoon)
2	teaspoons Hungarian paprika
1½	pounds Yukon Gold, Maine, or other all-purpose potatoes, peeled and cut into ¾-inch dice
1½	cups heavy whipping cream (or up to 2 cups if desired)
	Kosher or sea salt and freshly ground black pepper
2	tablespoons chopped fresh flat-leaf parsley
2	tablespoons minced fresh chives

Fill an 8- to 10-quart stockpot two-thirds full with water and salt it heavily. Bring to a rolling boil. Arrange several baking sheets near the stovetop. Carefully drop 1 lobster head-first into the water. Cook for exactly 4 minutes. (The lobster is only partially cooked so the meat can finish cooking in the chowder.) Using tongs, remove the lobster from the pot and set it on one of the nearby baking sheets. Repeat until all are cooked, and let them cool to room temperature. Pick all the meat from the tails, knuckles, and claws. Remove the intestinal tract from the tail. Cut the meat into ¾-inch dice. Cover and refrigerate until ready to use. Allow 1½ hours to make the lobster stock.

To make the stock: Split the lobster carcasses lengthwise and remove the head sac from each one. Place the carcasses, shells, and tomalley (the soft green substance in the body cavity) in a large stockpot, add the water, and bring to a boil, skimming the foam from the surface. (Using a

continued

ladle and a circular motion, push the foam from the center to the outside of the pot, where it is easy to remove.) Reduce the heat to a fast, steady simmer. Add the wine, tomatoes, onions, celery, carrots, garlic, thyme, bay leaves, fennel seeds, and peppercorns. Simmer for about 1 hour, or until flavorful. Add a little water if the stock falls below the lobster shells. Season with salt. Strain through a fine-mesh sieve. You should have 4 cups of stock. If not using within the hour, stir over ice to cool, then cover and refrigerate.

Christmas Tree Inn

To finish the chowder, heat a large, heavy pot over low heat and add the bacon. Once it has rendered a few tablespoons of fat, increase the heat to medium and cook until the bacon is a crisp golden brown. Pour off all but 1 tablespoon of the fat, leaving the bacon in the pot. Add the butter, onion, and thyme and sauté, stirring occasionally, for about 8 minutes, or until the onion is softened but not browned. Stir in the paprika and cook 1 minute longer.

Add the potatoes and lobster stock. (The stock should just barely cover the potatoes; if it doesn't, add enough water to cover.) Increase the heat to high and bring to a boil. Cover the pot and cook the potatoes vigorously for about 12 minutes, or until they are soft on the outside but still firm in the center. If the stock hasn't thickened slightly, smash a few potatoes against the side of the pot and cook for a minute or two longer to release their starch.

Remove the pot from the heat, stir in the reserved lobster meat and cream, and season with salt and pepper. (If not serving the chowder within the hour, let cool, then refrigerate; cover the chowder *after* it has chilled completely.) Otherwise, let it sit at room temperature for up to an hour, allowing the flavors to meld. To serve, reheat the chowder over low heat; don't let it boil. Use a slotted spoon to mound the lobster, onions, and potatoes in the center of some shallow bowls, making sure it is evenly divided, and ladle the creamy broth around. Sprinkle with the parsley and chives.

Serves 10 as a first course,
5 to 6 as a main course

Baked Christmas-Morning Oatmeal

John and Sallie Cwik, innkeepers at the Old Brick Inn at St. Michaels on the Eastern Shore, serve this hearty oatmeal to inn guests, and say it's one of their favorite Christmas Day breakfasts. Assemble all the ingredients the night before and refrigerate to let the flavors blend. Bake and serve with additional brown sugar and fresh fruit to convert even the most reluctant oatmeal opponents. Reheat leftovers in the microwave to keep the celebration going for several days.

2	cups old-fashioned rolled oats
1	cup steel-cut oats
½	cup packed brown sugar
½	cup maple syrup
¾	cup dried cherries, raisins, or fresh blueberries (optional)
½	cup slivered almonds (optional)
1	large unpeeled Granny Smith apple, cored and grated
2	teaspoons baking powder
1	teaspoon ground cinnamon
½	teaspoon ground nutmeg
½	teaspoon salt
1	teaspoon vanilla extract
3	cups milk
1	cup plain or vanilla yogurt
2	eggs, lightly beaten
2	tablespoons butter, melted

Lightly grease an 8-cup baking dish. Combine all the ingredients in a large bowl and stir until well mixed. Transfer to the prepared baking dish, cover tightly, and refrigerate overnight. In the morning, let the dish sit at room temperature for about 15 minutes. Heat the oven to 350°F and bake for 1 hour, or until the center feels set when you press it gently with a spoon. Serve hot, with milk, yogurt, and fresh fruit.

Serves 12 to 14

Note: Omit the brown sugar if you prefer oatmeal that isn't sweet.

THE BALTIMORE and OHIO'S FAMOUS "HOLLY TREE BY THE TRACKS" at JACKSON, MD.

Plum Pudding with Hard Sauce

English settlers to America brought along their tradition of serving holiday steamed pudding. This version, which uses cranberries, an old-time Massachusetts crop, can be served the very night you make it, or set aside to infuse with spirits to elevate the flavor. Don't fret about there being no plums in the ingredients list. Way back when, the word *plum* referred to raisins and other kinds of dried fruit.

'Merry Xmas

Heaps of pudding,
Heaps of Joy,
Heaps of Luck
for you old boy.

Grease and flour a 5- or 6-cup pudding mold or coffee can. Knock out the excess flour. Combine the flour, baking powder, baking soda, ginger, and cinnamon in a bowl and stir with a whisk to blend. Set aside. Cream the butter and sugars in a mixing bowl with an electric mixer. Beat in the egg, molasses, and orange zest. Add half of the dry ingredients, then half of the milk; repeat to add the remaining dry ingredients and milk, beating until the batter is smooth. Fold in the currants, apple, and cranberries. Turn the batter into the prepared mold and smooth the top. Cover the top of the pudding with a round of lightly greased

waxed paper, and cover the mold with a tight-fitting lid or a piece of greased aluminum foil tied tightly with string. Set the mold on a wire rack in a large pot and add water to three-fourths the depth of the mold. Bring the water just to a boil, reduce the heat to low. Cover the pot and steam for 2½ hours, checking the water level several times and adding more water as necessary. Remove the mold from the pot and let sit for 30 minutes.

To make the sauce: Combine all the ingredients in a food processor and blend until smooth. Run a knife around the edges of the pudding and unmold it onto a serving plate. Cut into wedge-

¾	cup all-purpose flour		¼	cup milk

¾ cup all-purpose flour

½ teaspoon baking powder

½ teaspoon baking soda

½ teaspoon ground ginger

½ teaspoon ground cinnamon

2 tablespoons butter at room temperature

¼ cup granulated sugar

¼ cup packed brown sugar

1 egg

¼ cup molasses

2 tablespoons grated orange zest

¼ cup milk

¼ cup dried currants

1 tart apple, peeled, cored, and chopped

1 cup fresh or frozen cranberries

Hard Sauce

½ cup (1 stick) butter at room temperature

1½ cups confectioners' sugar, sifted

2 teaspoons grated lemon or lime zest

1 tablespoon fresh lemon or lime juice

and serve warm with a dollop of hard sauce on top. Store any leftover hard sauce tightly covered in the refrigerator for up to 3 weeks, and store the pudding tightly covered at room temperature for up to 1 week.

Serves 6 to 8

Notes: If you wish to infuse your pudding with spirits, remove the mold from the water, let cool slightly, remove the lid or foil and waxed paper, and pour ¼ cup brandy over the top of the pudding. Re-cover and store in a cool, dry place for 2 to 3 weeks, adding 2 to 3 tablespoons brandy to the pudding once or twice a week. To serve, unmold the pudding onto a baking sheet, cover with foil, and reheat in a preheated 300°F oven for 30 to 40 minutes. Transfer the pudding to a platter and serve topped with hard sauce.

Shop for a pudding mold at your local cookware shop, or order online from www.kingarthurflour.com, www.fantes.com, or www.lacuisineus.com.

MERRY CHRISTMAS AND HAPPY NEW YEAR

ANN ARBOR MICH.

DIAGONAL WALKS
UNIVERSITY of MICHIGAN

Minty Cherry Carrots

By the early 1900s, Michigan's cherry industry was well established in orchards along the lake, and today the state produces about 75 percent of the tart cherries grown in the United States. Here, they're used to bring color and flavor to cooked carrots, in a recipe that's easy to double if you're feeding a gang. Make this dish a day ahead and simply reheat it in the microwave. The carrots remain wonderfully crunchy. Serve with any holiday main course.

Slice the carrots on the extreme diagonal into large, oval-shaped pieces and set aside. Melt the butter in a large frying pan over medium heat and sauté the onion for about 5 minutes, or until soft. Add the ginger and cook for 2 minutes longer. Add the carrots to the pan along with the water, maple syrup, and cherries. Stir gently to mix and cook, uncovered, for 30 minutes, stirring occasionally, until the carrots are crisp-tender. Sprinkle with the mint. Increase the heat to high and cook for 1 or 2 minutes, stirring gently. Serve hot.

Serves 6 as a side dish

5 to 6	large carrots, peeled
2	tablespoons butter
1	small onion, diced
1	tablespoon grated fresh ginger
½	cup water
3	tablespoons maple syrup, preferably Grade B (dark)
½	cup dried tart cherries
2	tablespoons chopped fresh mint

HOMEOPATHIC HOSPITAL

A MERRY CHRISTMAS AND A HAPPY
NEW YEAR · UNIVERSITY
OF MICHIGAN.

A merry
Christmas
to you

Roast Turkey with Herb Stuffing

Minnesota farmers raise a lot of turkeys, more than 44½ million each year, making their state the top turkey producer in the nation. Some 22 million turkeys turn up on Christmas tables in the United States. Here's a classic roast turkey with flavorful stuffing. Experiment with different types of fresh bread and combinations of herbs, nuts, and dried fruit to please your family and friends. Arrange slices of bread on a baking sheet the night before and leave out overnight to dry. Then pick it apart with your fingers. Start a tradition by assigning this task to older kids or spouses.

To make the stuffing: Combine the bread crumbs, pecans, and cranberries, if using, parsley, thyme, and tarragon in a large bowl and toss gently to mix. Set aside. Melt the butter with the olive oil in a large skillet over low heat. Add the onion and celery, increase the heat to medium, and sauté for 5 or 6 minutes, or until the vegetables are soft. Add the onion mixture to the bread crumb mixture and toss gently. Season with salt to taste.

It's Christmas in Minnesota

To roast the turkey: Heat the oven to 325°F. Rinse the turkey and pat it dry. Season the body cavity and outside of the bird with salt and pepper to taste. Spoon the stuffing loosely into the cavity and sew the bird closed with a large needle and kitchen twine. Place the turkey, breast side up, on a flat wire rack in a roasting pan. Brush or rub the turkey all over with the oil or butter.

Bake the turkey for about 3½ hours, tenting with aluminum foil after 2 hours to prevent overbrowning and help keep the breast meat from drying out. Using an instant-read thermometer, check the turkey after 2½ hours; it is done when it reaches 170°F in the thickest part of the breast, 180°F in the thigh.

Remove the turkey from the oven and let it sit for 10 minutes so the juices drain into the roasting pan. Transfer the turkey to a platter and let it sit for 10 minutes before carving. While the turkey sits, make the gravy.

Herb Stuffing

4	cups coarse white and/or whole-wheat bread crumbs
½	cup chopped pecans (optional)
½	cup dried cranberries or currants (optional)
¼	cup chopped fresh flat-leaf parsley
2	teaspoons dried thyme
1	tablespoon dried tarragon
4	tablespoons butter
2	tablespoons olive oil
1	large onion, diced
2	stalks celery, diced
	Salt
1	turkey, 12 to 14 pounds
	Salt and freshly ground pepper
2	tablespoons olive oil or melted butter
	About 2 cups chicken broth or water
3	tablespoons all-purpose flour

To make the gravy: Pour the broth or water into a medium saucepan and keep warm over low heat. Pour all of the drippings from the pan into a gravy separator or small bowl and let sit for several minutes to allow the fat to rise to the top. Leave all the browned bits in the roasting pan and set it on the stove top. Remove as much fat as possible from the drippings and pour back into the roasting pan. Stirring with a whisk to loosen all the bits in the pan, bring the drippings to a boil. Sprinkle the flour over and cook, whisking constantly, until thickened and smooth. (If lumps persist, strain the gravy at the very end of the process.) Add about ½ cup of the hot broth or water and whisk it into the gravy. When the gravy bubbles, add another ½ cup of the broth or water and continue until all has been used. Let the gravy bubble for several minutes to thicken. If too thick, add a bit more broth or water to reach the desired consistency. Season with salt and pepper and serve hot in a gravy boat. If possible, leave some of the gravy in the pan to be reheated quickly for seconds.

Serves 10 to 12

Variations: Save the water used to cook potatoes and use in place of the chicken broth or water.

Combine the flour with 3 tablespoons warm water in a small jar with a tight-fitting lid. Shake it vigorously until smooth and add to the pan juices in thirds, whisking the gravy as it thickens.

For a chestnut-herb stuffing, omit the pecans, increase the amount of butter by 2 tablespoons, sauté about ½ cup chestnuts (see page 62) along with the onion and celery, and reduce the amount of bread by about ½ cup.

Seafood Spread

Mississippi has long been a rich source of shrimp, oysters, and crabs. In the 1900s, with railroads to ship its seafood and factories to can it, Biloxi was known as the Seafood Capital of the World. Biloxi butter, a mixture of shrimp, cream cheese, butter, and garlic powder, is one of its legacies. At Christmastime, seafood spreads and dips are popular party fare throughout the state. This version uses the tasty combination of shrimp and crabmeat.

Combine the cream cheese, mayonnaise, Worcestershire sauce, and cocktail sauce in a food processor and blend until smooth. Add the shrimp and crabmeat and pulse for just a second. The mixture should be slightly chunky, not smooth. Transfer to a bowl and stir in the chives and pimientos. Refrigerate overnight and serve cold, or heat in the microwave for about 1 minute and serve hot, with crackers.

Makes 2 cups

One	8-ounce package cream cheese at room temperature
2	tablespoons mayonnaise
1	teaspoon Worcestershire sauce
1	teaspoon cocktail sauce
2	cups chopped cooked shrimp (about 1 pound, or 35 medium shrimp)
6	ounces lump or canned crabmeat, drained
2	tablespoons minced fresh chives
2	tablespoons diced pimientos

*DECEMBER 25 * 1943*

2nd MESS GROUP

Christmas GREETINGS

KEESLER FIELD * MISS.

Oven-Roasted Chestnut Appetizers

At this time of year, we'll all hear the refrain "chestnuts roasting on an open fire." Julie Rhoads, events coordinator at the University of Missouri Center for Agroforestry, has gone much further, and figured out *the* way to shell and roast chestnuts with the least fuss and the best flavor. She has served the sweet, starchy Missouri-grown nuts—more akin to potatoes or grains than other nuts— to visitors at the annual Missouri Chestnut Roast in New Franklin. This holiday season, pass around a tray of them and ask friends to guess what you're serving.

Using a hand pruner rather than a knife, cut the chestnuts in half. Here are two ways to remove the meat from the shells:

Steaming method: Place the cut chestnuts in a steaming basket and place the basket in a pan of water about ½-inch deep. Bring the water to a boil, cover the pan, and steam for about 5 minutes, or until the meats separate easily from the shells

1   pound shelled raw chestnut meats
About 3 tablespoons olive oil
Seasoned salt

and the chestnuts are slightly cooked but still crunchy. If you want soft chestnuts, continue steaming until they reach the desired consistency.

Microwave method: Add a small amount of water to a glass baking dish, spread the cut chestnuts out in a single layer, and microwave for 1 minute on high. Check to see if the meats have separated from the shells; if not, microwave for 1 minute more. Many of the meats will separate on their own; for those that don't separate completely, squeeze on the edges of the shell, and the meat should pop out. The meats are not cooked at this point; boil or bake to make them soft enough to use in recipes calling for chestnuts.

Heat the oven to 250°F. Put the shelled chestnuts in a bowl and drizzle with the olive oil. Toss to

coat. Arrange in a single layer on a baking sheet and sprinkle with seasoned salt to taste. Bake for 20 to 30 minutes, or until slightly crunchy. Let cool slightly. Insert a toothpick into each piece and serve warm.

Serves 6 to 8

Note: Store unshelled chestnuts in a plastic bag in the refrigerator for up to 3 or 4 weeks.

Venison Steaks au Poivre

If you have a hunter in your household, you might have venison on your holiday menu, a Christmas tradition that dates back decades in the American West. This quick-cooking recipe, which keeps the meat tender, was created by Larry Copenhaver, who, after a seventeen-year cooking career, joined the staff at the Montana Wildlife Federation. MWF was a primary facilitator of a statewide initiative to outlaw shooting operations on game farms, and Larry urges cooks who don't know a hunter to make this recipe with beef strip loin or buffalo steak instead of farmed venison. To get the pepper just right, put whole black peppercorns into a self-sealing plastic bag and crack them with a mallet. Serve with baby peas and sautéed mushrooms.

Lay a piece of aluminum foil out on the counter and spread the pepper on it. Dredge the steaks in the pepper, which can be liberally applied but shouldn't totally encrust the meat. With the hood vent on and perhaps a window open, melt the butter in a skillet over medium-high heat and sear the peppered steaks for 2 minutes on each side, or until medium-rare (145°F). Transfer the steaks to a platter and return the pan to medium-high heat. Add the rosemary, sage, and brandy and stir to scrape up the browned bits from the bottom of the pan. Simmer until reduced by about two-thirds. Add the mustards and whisk until the sauce is smooth and just starting to brown. Add the cream, stir well, and bring to a low boil.

¼	cup cracked black peppercorns
2	venison round or tenderloin steaks, about 10 ounces each
3	tablespoons butter
¼	teaspoon crushed dried rosemary
¼	teaspoon ground dried sage
⅓	cup brandy
2	tablespoons stone-ground mustard
2	tablespoons Dijon mustard
1	cup heavy cream

A Christmas Feast Assured, Venison for dinner in the Rockies of Montana

8884 Christmas Tree Park, Yellowstone National Park.

Reduce the heat to medium-low and cook, whisking frequently, until reduced by about half. (Keep an eye on the sauce and don't reduce it too much, or it will clump and separate.)

Return the meat to the pan and turn to coat it with sauce. If you prefer a more done steak, cook in the sauce until the desired doneness (160°F for medium, 170°F for well done).

Serves 4

Roast Beef with Yorkshire Pudding

From the mid-1950s to the mid-1960s, Nebraska license plates proudly claimed theirs as the Beef State. In a land where cattle outnumber residents four to one, Christmas is traditionally celebrated with a standing rib roast. Buy the best roast you can, allowing about four ribs for six people, which will give you plenty of leftovers for sandwiches. Cook the Yorkshire Pudding as you let the roast sit before carving.

1	beef rib roast (5 to 6 pounds)
	Salt and freshly ground pepper

Yorkshire Pudding

2	eggs
1	cup milk
1	cup all-purpose flour
½	teaspoon salt

Remove the meat from the refrigerator about 2 hours before cooking. Heat the oven to 350°F. Place the meat in a large roasting pan, bone side down, and season liberally with salt and pepper to taste. Cook for 20 minutes per pound (1 hour and 40 minutes to 2 hours) for medium-rare (130°F to 140°F), checking the temperature with an instant-read thermometer after 1 hour. Remove the roast from the oven and let stand for 20 minutes before carving. To serve, slice the meat across the grain, using a very sharp knife.

To make the Yorkshire Pudding: About 10 minutes before the roast is done, combine all the ingredients in a bowl and whisk until smooth. Set aside. When the roast is done, increase the oven temperature to 450°F. Pour 3 to 4 tablespoons of drippings from the roasting pan into a 7-by-11-inch baking pan. Whisk the pudding ingredients once more and pour evenly into the pan. Bake for 25 to 30 minutes, or until the pudding is puffy and brown. Cut into squares and serve alongside the roast beef.

Serves 6 to 8

Variation: To make the roast slightly crispy on the outside, heat the oven to 450°F and cook the roast for 15 minutes. Reduce the temperature to 350°F and cook about 1 hour and 45 minutes longer for medium-rare.

Christmas Recipes

1953

"The GAS Company"

CENTRAL ELECTRIC & GAS COMPANY

Onion Soup Gratinée

Las Vegas is a popular holiday destination for regulars from around the world who fill the casinos and restaurants. In addition to roast beef, visitors can count on finding onion soup on just about every Christmas dinner menu. It's easy to spark a debate about who in town serves the best bowl. Put this soup on the menu for your family dinner, or serve it for a special lunch when everyone has time to linger at the table. Make it a day in advance and refrigerate until ready to serve. Then reheat slowly and top with the bread and cheese.

The same old Santa
And the same old wreath
With the same old greeting
underneath.
A Merry Christmas.

4	tablespoons butter
2	large sweet white onions, very thinly sliced
2	tablespoons sugar
⅓	cup dry white wine
8	cups beef broth or a mixture of beef and chicken broth
1	sprig fresh thyme
1	bay leaf
	Salt and freshly ground pepper
6 to 8	slices French bread
1½	cups shredded Gruyère or Emmental cheese

Melt the butter in a large pot over medium-low heat, add the onions, and cook, stirring frequently, for 30 minutes, or until very soft and lightly browned. Add the sugar and cook for several minutes. Add the wine and stir gently. Increase the heat to medium-high and cook for 2 minutes longer. Add the broth, thyme, and bay leaf, reduce the heat to medium, and simmer for 1 hour. Season with salt and pepper to taste.

Lightly toast the bread slices. Remove the thyme and bay leaf from the soup. Ladle the soup into heatproof bowls, top with a slice of toasted bread, and sprinkle the bread with cheese to taste. Run the bowls under the broiler for a few minutes until the cheese is melted. Serve immediately.

Serves 6 to 8 as a first course

Snowballs

Also known as Russian tea cakes, these easy-to-make but delectable cookies are one of the signature treats served at the Darby Field Inn in Albany, New Hampshire, during the annual December Inn to Inn Cookie Tour. Seventeen New Hampshire inns decorated for the holidays offer their own special cookies and candies, plus plenty of ideas for home bakers. Visitors to all seventeen inns are awarded a special prize.

Heat the oven to 350°F. Put 1 cup of the sugar into a shallow bowl and reserve. Cream the butter in a mixing bowl with an electric mixer. Add the remaining 1 cup sugar and the vanilla and beat until smooth. With the mixer on low speed, gradually add the flour, salt, and pecans and mix just until the dough holds together. Shape the dough into 1-inch balls and place about 1 inch apart on an ungreased baking sheet. Bake for 17 to 20 minutes, or until set but not browned.

Remove from the oven and let sit on the baking sheet for 10 minutes. Roll in the reserved confectioners' sugar while still slightly warm and set on a wire rack. When completely cool, roll

2	cups confectioners' sugar, sifted
1	cup (2 sticks) butter, softened
1½	teaspoons vanilla extract
2¼	cups all-purpose flour
¾	teaspoon salt
1	cup finely chopped pecans

in the sugar again. Store in an airtight container for up 2 weeks.

Makes 2½ dozen

SANTA'S VILLAGE

HOME OF SANTA AND HIS HELPERS

A Village of Enchantment in the White Mountains

JEFFERSON, NEW HAMPSHIRE

on Route 2

ON THE PRESIDENTIAL HIGHWAY
IN THE CHRISTMAS TREE COUNTRY

Something new for kids of all ages . . .

Don't miss Santa's Village

Now you can visit everybody's favorite—Santa Claus—in his own home. See him! Talk with him! See his Village and his helpers at work.

In the heart of the White Mountains at Jefferson, N. H. is Santa's Village. The quaint, rustic houses of the village are a colorful sight nestled among the mountain pines. As you walk up the shaded road from the parking lot you are welcomed first by Santa's Monkey Band in the music house. Their cheery, syncopated greeting welcomes you to the Village. Next there is Santa's Post Office where cards and letters may be mailed. Santa's house is next and there he is usually to be found, relaxing on the porch and talking to the many daily visitors. The toy workshops are next on our tour through the Village—here Santa's helpers are busy with their summer tasks.

Throughout the natural setting of Santa's Village, deer, baby lambs and goats roam. They are great favorites with the children and they like to have their pictures taken. There are several good spots for vacation photos—in Santa's sleigh or beside the igloo and north pole. Near the dairy bar is the pond where the white ducks paddle lazily around—and of course they have a house too. Across the bridge, over the duck pond is a shrine to our Saviour—whose birthday is Christmas. The wishing well—where all children make a wish and toss in a coin—is a means of providing underprivileged children with gifts at Christmas. *Artists for the Village are Miss Patricia Beecher and the Cardinal Brothers of Lancaster.*

WINTER IN THE WHITE MOUNTAINS OF NEW HAMPSHIRE   500L

Christmas Pea Salad

From the lights on the exterior to the decorations inside, the Garden State's Queen Victoria B&B on Cape May is a charming place to stay during the holidays. Every year, innkeepers Doug and Anna McMain decorate at least five Christmas trees: two with their own family ornaments, and one early Victorian (1840s), one mid-Victorian (1870s), and one late Victorian (1890s). Karen Andrus, who once ran a catering business on Cape May, created this colorful dish, which has become a favorite on Christmas Eve at Queen Victoria. The McMains say that it is their most-requested holiday recipe.

Two	10-ounce packages frozen peas
1/4	cup canola oil
1 1/2	tablespoons apple cider vinegar
2	tablespoons chopped scallion
2	tablespoons finely chopped sweet pickles
2	tablespoons finely chopped pimientos
1	teaspoon salt
1/2	teaspoon freshly ground pepper

Put the peas in a large bowl and pour a kettle of boiling water over them. Drain well. Refrigerate for about 30 minutes, or until chilled. Add all the remaining ingredients to the peas and toss. Refrigerate for at least 2 hours. Toss lightly with a fork before serving.

Serves 8 to 10 as a side dish

Biscochitos

Traditionally found on New Mexico holiday tables and served at celebrations following the lighting of the luminarias on Christmas Eve, these flaky treats spiced with anise are so popular they have been declared the official state cookie. From the cuisine of New Mexico's early Spanish settlers, authentic *biscochitos* are made with lard. Do not refrigerate this dough. It must be warm to hold together.

A New Mexico Christmas.

My Holly is the Chili red
  Upon the wall displayed
My Christmas Tree are Mountain Piñon
  In glittering Dews arrayed

My Candles are a thousand Stars
  In GOD'S eternal Skies
My Psalms the distant whisperings
  That from the Woods arise

My dearest Christmas Gift tonight
  Is the Love of Those I Love
Which East, or West, or Anywhere
  Is Christmas Gift Enough!

Elwood M. Albright

Cinnamon Sugar

¼	cup sugar
1	tablespoon ground cinnamon
3	cups all-purpose flour
1½	teaspoons baking powder
½	teaspoon salt
¾	cup sugar
½	cup vegetable shortening (preferably nonhydrogenated) or lard
1	egg
1½	teaspoons vanilla extract
1	teaspoon anise seed

Heat the oven to 325°F. Lightly oil a baking sheet.

To make the cinnamon sugar: Combine the sugar and the cinnamon in a small bowl and stir until blended. Set aside.

To make the biscochitos: Combine the flour, baking powder, and salt in a medium bowl and stir with a whisk to blend. Set aside. Combine the sugar and the shortening in a mixing bowl and beat on medium speed until creamy. Add the egg,

beat until smooth. Add the dry ingredients to the sugar mixture a little at a time, beating well after each addition, to make a crumbly dough.

Pull off a tennis-ball-size amount of dough and place it on a lightly floured surface. Working slowly but firmly, roll the dough out to the thickness of a pie crust. (Keep your fingers on the top of the rolling pin and use light, short strokes.) Using a sharp knife or a cookie cutter, cut the dough into desired shapes. Dust the cookies with cinnamon sugar and place on the prepared pan. Bake for 10 to 15 minutes, or until the edges are just slightly brown. Transfer the cookies to a wire rack and let cool.

Makes 3 to 4 dozen, depending on shape

Oyster Stew

When the Dutch arrived in New York in the seventeenth century, they found rich oyster beds in the estuary of the lower Hudson River, and for several centuries oysters were harvested from all of today's boroughs. Those from the East River and Staten Island were among the finest in the world, shipped to London and Paris. In 1927, city officials closed the last New York oyster bed, off Staten Island, but New Yorkers never fell out of love with the briny cold-water delicacies.

In 1949, when Mary I. van der Ploeg moved from England to America with her Dutch husband, she was served oyster stew at her first holiday dinner party in New York. She was so taken with it that she developed this recipe and made it an annual affair for her family. Easy to prepare but hauntingly delicious, it's a good choice for a Christmas Eve or New Year's Eve supper. For an even richer version, substitute ½ cup heavy whipping cream for ½ cup of the milk.

Pour the oysters into a shallow bowl and pick through them to remove any bits of shell. Melt the butter in a medium saucepan over low heat. Add the oysters and their liquor and cook over low heat, stirring gently, for about 5 minutes, or until the edges just begin to curl. While the oysters cook, pour the milk into a saucepan and bring just to a simmer over medium-low heat. Add the scalded milk and seasonings to the oysters. Serve immediately.

Serves 4 as a main course

1	pint shucked oysters with their liquor (about 2 dozen oysters)
4	tablespoons butter
4	cups whole milk
¼	teaspoon celery salt
½	teaspoon Worcestershire sauce

Court Square

Wishing You A Merry Christmas From Binghamton, N. Y.

WILSER The SEASON'S GREETINGS From HALF MOON LAKE HOTEL

3A-H621

Christmas Greetings from the Land of Liberty.

NORTH POLE, N.Y.

HOME OF SANTA'S WORKSHOP

North Carolina

Sweet Potato Pudding

Community Christmas Tree, Wilmington, North Carolina

North Carolina is the country's leading producer of sweet potatoes. In 1993, the tuber was named the official state vegetable. It graces many a holiday table, especially in the South, where one traditional side dish calls for raw potatoes to be grated, sweetened, and baked into a custard. This version, which contains very little sugar, is easy to make ahead and reheat. Or, bake the sweet potatoes, let them cool, and refrigerate them in their skins for up to two days before you assemble the pudding.

4	orange-fleshed sweet potatoes
3	tablespoons butter
4	tablespoons packed brown sugar
½	teaspoon ground cinnamon
½	teaspoon ground ginger
¼	teaspoon freshly grated nutmeg
1	tablespoon dark rum
	Salt and freshly ground pepper
3	tablespoons chopped pecans

Heat the oven to 400°F. Grease an 8-cup soufflé or baking dish and set aside. Place the sweet potatoes in a shallow baking dish and bake for 45 minutes, or until fork-tender. Let cool for 10 minutes, or until you can handle them. Turn the oven temperature down to 350°F. Cut the sweet potatoes in half lengthwise and scoop the flesh out into a bowl. Mash it lightly. Discard the skins. Stir in the butter, 2 tablespoons of the brown sugar, the cinnamon, ginger, nutmeg, and rum. Season with salt and pepper to taste.

Transfer the mixture to the prepared soufflé dish. Combine the remaining 2 tablespoons brown sugar with the pecans in a small bowl and mix with your fingertips or a fork. Sprinkle the mixture over the pudding. Bake for 30 minutes, or until lightly browned.

Serves 8 to 10 as a side dish

Cranberry Scones

Farmers in North Dakota grow more than half of all the high-protein hard red spring wheat produced in the United States and over 70 percent of the country's durum wheat crop. They make enough of the former, prized by bakers for its gluten content, to produce 14.3 billion loaves of bread, and of the latter, used for pasta, to provide 13.7 billion servings of spaghetti. Chances are that the all-purpose flour you buy for your Christmas cookies will contain some wheat from North Dakota. Include a batch or two of these scones in your holiday baking. They come together quickly and taste especially wonderful hot from the oven. Serve with coffee or tea.

1¾	cups all-purpose flour
3	tablespoons sugar
2½	teaspoons baking powder
½	teaspoon salt
5	tablespoons cold butter, cut into bits
2	eggs
½	cup dried cranberries
4 to 6	tablespoons half-and-half

Heat the oven to 400°F. Combine the flour, sugar, baking powder, and salt in a mixing bowl and stir with a whisk to blend. Using a pastry cutter, a fork, or your fingertips, cut the butter into the flour mixture until it resembles fine crumbs. Beat 1 of the eggs and add it to the crumbs along with the cranberries. Add enough half-and-half, stirring the mixture gently, to form a soft dough that pulls away from the sides of the bowl. Turn the dough out onto a lightly floured surface. Knead lightly 10 times. Roll or pat out into a round about 10 inches across and ½ inch thick. Cut the round in half, then into quarters, and then into eighths, creating 8 pie-shaped pieces. Place the pieces on an ungreased baking sheet. Beat the remaining egg and brush it on the dough.

Bake for 10 to 12 minutes, or until golden brown. Serve hot. Let leftover scones cool completely and store in an airtight container for up to 2 days. To heat, split in half, toast, and spread with butter.

Makes 8

Variation: Substitute ½ cup raisins, dried blueberries, chopped nuts, or chopped candied ginger for the cranberries.

Chex Party Mix

The recipe for this classic snack, using cereal made in Ohio, first appeared on the side panel of a Chex box in 1953. It has become a perennial holiday favorite for many families. Variations abound. General Mills cereal box recipes call for bagel chips, which weren't available when the mix was first introduced. The classic recipe from the 1950s uses three kinds of Chex cereal, along with pretzel sticks and mixed nuts. Try different small pretzel shapes, or upgrade the nuts to all pecans for a premier blend. As you combine the ingredients in the baking pan, tailor the quantities of pretzels and nuts as you wish. Stored in an airtight container, the mix will keep for several weeks—but it's unlikely it will be around that long.

Heat the oven to 250°F. Cut the butter into chunks, drop them into a 10-by-15-inch baking pan, and put the pan in the oven for about 5 minutes, or until the butter is melted. Add the salt, Worcestershire sauce, and onion and garlic powders, if using, and stir with a whisk to blend.

6	tablespoons butter
1	teaspoon seasoned salt
5	teaspoons Worcestershire sauce or soy sauce
½	teaspoon onion powder (optional)
½	teaspoon garlic powder (optional)
3	cups Corn Chex
3	cups Rice Chex
3	cups Wheat Chex
1 to 2	cups pretzel sticks
1 to 2	cups salted mixed nuts

Gradually add the remaining ingredients to the pan, tossing gently with a rubber spatula to mix evenly. Bake for 1 hour, stirring gently every 15 minutes. Let cool in the pan and then store in an airtight container.

Makes 11 to 13 cups

Variation: There's plenty of salt in this mix, which could prove problematic for anyone paying close attention to sodium consumption. Cut back by using unsalted butter, a salt-free seasoning blend in place of the seasoned salt, light soy sauce, and unsalted nuts.

Aunt Bill's Brown Candy

Helen Betty Townley first obtained the recipe for this delightful holiday treat from *Aunt Susan's Cooking School of the Air,* a popular radio show in Oklahoma City in the 1930s. (Its namesake remains a mystery.) With the texture of fudge and the taste of caramel, the candy soon became a family favorite, and by the time Cynthia Townley Ewer was born in 1954, it was a holiday tradition. Beginning in World War II,

the women in her family also have made batches to send to family members in the service. Cut into small pieces and wrapped in aluminum foil, it travels well, needs no refrigeration, and stays fresh for a long time. Cynthia recommends making this with one or two helpers; between pouring the melted sugar and beating the candy for close to 20 minutes, strong arms are always welcome.

Butter a 9-by-13-inch baking dish and set aside. Rub the inside of a large, heavy saucepan with butter. Add 4 cups of the sugar and the milk to the pan, stir, and set aside. Put the remaining 2 cups sugar in a large cast-iron skillet over medium heat. Stir constantly until the sugar starts to melt. When it begins to melt, in about 10 minutes, place the milk-sugar mixture over very low heat, stirring occasionally until the sugar dissolves. Keep warm.

Continue melting the sugar in the skillet, stirring, until caramelized to the color of light brown sugar. Melting sugar scorches very easily, so watch carefully. The entire process takes almost 30 minutes.

6	cups sugar
2	cups milk or half-and-half
1/4	teaspoon baking soda
1/2	cup (1 stick) butter
1	teaspoon vanilla extract
2	pounds pecans, broken (8 cups)

The next step requires family teamwork. Pour the caramelized sugar into the simmering milk mixture in a thin stream "no bigger than a knitting needle." Stir constantly! This step may take 5 minutes, and works best if someone strong pours the caramel

A Merry Christmas and a Happy New Year

MOONLIGHT ON THE ARKANSAS,
TULSA, OKLA.

Christmas Greetings

MAIN STREET
OKLAHOMA CITY, OKLA.

v·e·r·y s·l·o·w·l·y. Continue cooking the mixture to the firm-ball stage (246°F). Do not stir, other than to scrape the sides of the pan occasionally. Remove from the heat at once. Stir in the baking soda (the candy will foam vigorously, so call the children to watch this step). Plop the butter into the foaming mixture and let everything sit, without stirring, for 30 minutes.

Add the vanilla and beat with a wooden spoon, in turns with your helper, until the mixture stiffens and loses its gloss, 10 to 15 minutes. Add the pecans, stir to mix, and turn the candy out into the prepared pan. Let the candy cool until barely warm, and cut into small pieces. When cool, wrap each piece in aluminum foil or colored foil gift wrap and store in an airtight container for up to a month.

Makes about 4 dozen pieces

A Merry Christmas and a Happy New Year

OKLAHOMA CITY, OKLA.

Cherry-Chocolate Torte

In the mid-1800s, Oregon farmers started growing cherries, which thrived in the Willamette Valley's fertile soil, and climate of gentle spring rain and moderate summer weather. By the early twentieth century, most of the state's crop was being canned, and by 1930, Oregon had cornered the market for maraschino cherries. The tradition of canning fruit is carried on today by companies such as Oregon Fruit in Salem, a third-generation family-owned-and-operated company. This luscious dessert is one of their special recipes.

To make the cake: Heat the oven to 350°F. Lightly grease an 8-inch round cake pan, line with a round of waxed paper, grease the paper lightly, and set aside. Combine the almonds and sugar in a food processor and blend until finely ground. Set aside. Cream the butter in a mixing bowl with an electric mixer until light. Beat in the egg yolks, one at a time, until well mixed. Add the melted chocolate and beat until smooth. Add the almond mixture to the chocolate mixture along with the bread crumbs and beat on low speed just until combined.

Cake
¾ cup (3 ounces) whole raw almonds
½ cup sugar
½ cup (1 stick) butter, softened
3 eggs, separated
½ cup semisweet chocolate chips or chunks, melted
¼ cup dried bread crumbs
⅛ teaspoon cream of tartar
Pinch of salt

Topping
One 15-ounce can Oregon pitted dark sweet cherries with syrup
¾ cup heavy whipping cream
6 ounces bittersweet chocolate, chopped
White chocolate for curls (optional)

In a mixing bowl, beat the egg whites with the cream of tartar and salt until stiff, glossy peaks form. Fold the egg whites into the cake batter and pour into the prepared pan. Bake for 25 to 30 minutes, or until a toothpick inserted in the center comes out clean. Let cool in the pan for 15 minutes and then invert onto a wire rack to cool completely.

To make the topping: Pour the cherries into a sieve set over a bowl and let drain for 20 minutes.

Reserve 1 tablespoon of the syrup. Heat the cream in a saucepan over medium heat just until it begins to boil. Remove the pan from the heat and add the chocolate and reserved syrup. Let sit for 3 minutes. Stir to combine. Let cool for 15 minutes and then pour over the cooled cake. Arrange the cherries on top of the chocolate. Decorate with white chocolate curls, if desired, and refrigerate until ready to serve.

Serves 8 to 10

Amish Christmas Caramel Corn

Known for their neat-as-a-pin houses and devotion to farming, the Amish make a serious commitment to separate themselves from the modern material world, using horses and buggies rather than cars, and running households without electricity. The women, who wear long skirts, celebrate the holiday season by making numerous treats, among them this tasty popcorn snack. Once you sample it, you will never again want to buy caramel corn from a store. If you don't have two deep roasting or baking pans, buy two disposable aluminum foil pans large enough so you can stir the baking popcorn without sending it all over the kitchen.

1⅔	cups popcorn kernels (12 ounces)
2	cups dry-roasted peanuts (optional)
2	cups packed brown sugar
½	cup light corn syrup
1	teaspoon salt
1	cup (2 sticks) butter
½	teaspoon baking soda
1	teaspoon vanilla extract

Pop the corn in a saucepan or popper according to package directions. Put the popped corn in 2 greased deep baking or roasting pans. Add the peanuts, if using. Set aside. Heat the oven to 250°F. Combine the brown sugar, corn syrup, salt, and butter in a large saucepan. Bring to a boil over medium heat, stirring until blended. Continue cooking for 5 minutes, stirring constantly.

Remove the pan from the heat. Add the baking soda and vanilla and stir until light and foamy. Immediately pour the syrup over the popcorn in the pans and stir until the popcorn is well coated.

(Don't worry about coating every bit of popcorn; there is ample opportunity to coat it with syrup during the subsequent stirrings.) Transfer the pans to the oven and bake for 1 hour, removing the pans to stir every 15 minutes or so.

Line the counter with waxed paper. Dump the coated popcorn out onto the waxed paper and gently separate the pieces with a rubber spatula.

Let cool completely. Store in resealable plastic bags or airtight containers for up to 3 weeks.

Makes about 7 quarts

Note: Yoder Lady Finger popcorn is a favored Amish brand for this recipe. Made from the smallest kernels you can buy, it pops up hulless and absolutely melts in your mouth. Visit www.yoderpopcorn.com.

Tourtière

In the 1840s, large numbers of French Canadians were recruited from Quebec to work in Rhode Island's textile mills. By 1842, Woonsocket alone boasted 20 mills, and today French Canadians remain the town's largest ethnic group. On Christmas Eve, many families still gather to eat *tourtière,* a savory pie made with pork and beef. Some old-timers recommend making the pie ahead of time and reheating it for the best flavor. There are many versions, some with potatoes, some without, all made according to treasured family recipes, as evidenced by the spirited Tourtière Contest held each year in Woonsocket. Debated accompaniments include ketchup and/or sweet pickles. This recipe was created by Sue Gray, director of the test kitchen for King Arthur Flour, for her husband, Mike, who grew up in Lincoln, just down the road from Woonsocket.

CALL AT THE GREAT
5 & 10 Cent Store,
13 Westminster Street,
PROVIDENCE, R. I.

Pastry

¾	cup lard or vegetable shortening (preferably nonhydrogenated)
⅓	cup boiling water
2¼	cups all-purpose flour
1½	teaspoons baking powder
½	teaspoon salt

Filling

1	teaspoon salt
2	cups water
4 to 5	potatoes, peeled and cut into ½-inch dice (2½ cups)
½	pound ground beef
½	pound ground pork
1	cup chopped onion
1	cup chopped celery
2	cloves garlic, minced
¼	teaspoon ground cloves
1	teaspoon ground thyme
½	teaspoon ground sage
1	teaspoon freshly ground pepper

To make the pastry: Put the lard in a mixing bowl, add the boiling water, and stir well to melt the fat. Add the flour, baking powder, and salt and mix with a spoon or electric mixer to make a smooth dough. Scrape half of the dough out of the bowl onto a piece of plastic wrap, form it into a disk, and wrap well. Repeat with the remaining dough, and refrigerate both dough disks while preparing the filling.

To make the filling: Combine the salt, water, and potatoes in a medium saucepan and bring to a boil over medium heat. Cook until the potatoes are fork-tender, about 10 minutes. Drain, reserving the water, and set aside.

Brown the meats over medium-high heat in a large frying pan. Drain off the excess fat. Add the onion, celery, garlic, spices, and reserved potato water to the meat. Bring to a boil, then reduce the heat to medium-low and simmer, stirring occasionally, for 30 minutes, or until the liquid

has evaporated and the vegetables are tender. Mash about half of the potato chunks and add them to the meat. Gently stir in the remaining chunks of potato. Remove from the heat and let cool to room temperature.

To assemble the *tourtière*: Heat the oven to 450°F. Take one piece of dough out of the refrigerator, unwrap it, and dust both sides with flour. Roll it out to about ¼ inch thick (or less if you prefer a thinner crust). Line a 9-inch pie pan with the dough and fill it with the cooled meat mixture. Roll out the remaining dough disk and place it over the filling. Trim the excess from the dough and crimp the edges together with a fork or your fingers. Bake for 15 minutes. Reduce the oven temperature to 350°F and bake for 30 minutes, or until golden brown. Let cool for at least 15 minutes before slicing.

Makes 1 pie; serves 8 to 10

Ambrosia

This popular Southern fruit salad is a must on many holiday tables, although it appears in many forms. Traditionalists insist on cracking fresh coconuts and using fresh pineapple, while cooks in a hurry rely on dried coconut and canned fruit. For best results, make it exactly the way your Mama did, and double the recipe. However you make it, it's one of the first things to disappear.

Peel the oranges and pull them into segments, working over a bowl to catch all the juice and dropping them into the bowl as you go. Add the pineapple and sugar to taste and toss gently to blend. Arrange about one-third of the fruit in a glass bowl. Top with about one-third of the coconut. Repeat the layers, ending by scattering coconut on the top. Cover with plastic wrap and refrigerate for at least 1 hour before serving.

Serves 6 to 8

Variations: Add 2 red grapefruits, peeled and sectioned, along with the oranges.

Mix whipped cream or sour cream into the salad.

6	large oranges, or 3 cans mandarin oranges, drained
1	pineapple, peeled, cored, and cut into cubes, or one 20-ounce can pineapple chunks, drained
2	tablespoons confectioners' sugar
1	cup freshly grated coconut, or ½ to 1 cup sweetened flaked coconut

Serve topped with sweetened whipped cream as a dessert.

Season's
Greetings

U. S. NAVAL HOSPITAL
CHARLESTON, S. C.

Kathryn's Roast Goose Supreme with Sage Stuffing and Plum Sauce

In 1944, Kathryn Schiltz gave her husband, Marlin, several goose eggs. He hatched two of them into goslings that he sold for 12 cents a pound, and the family business was begun. Today, Schiltz Foods, headquartered in Sisseton, is the largest goose producer in America. For anyone who plans to roast a goose this holiday season, here's *the* way to do it, from the kitchens of Kathryn Schiltz and her daughter-in-law, Marcia Schiltz. When buying a goose, allow 1½ pounds frozen weight for each serving.

Thaw a frozen goose in the refrigerator, allowing 1 to 2 days, depending on the size of the bird. To hasten the process, thaw it at room temperature in a large pot of cold water for 4 to 8 hours.

Heat the oven to 350°F. Remove the neck and giblets from the body cavity. Remove the excess fat from the body cavity and neck skin, rinse the bird, and drain. Prick the entire goose several

1	goose, 13 to 14 pounds

Marcia's Sage Stuffing

1	loaf slightly stale white or whole-wheat bread
3	tablespoons butter
1	onion, diced
1	cup diced celery
4	eggs, lightly beaten
4	cups chicken broth
	Salt and freshly ground pepper
	About 2 tablespoons dried sage

Kathryn's Plum Sauce

2	cups fresh, frozen, or canned plums with juice, pitted and halved or quartered
¼	cup sugar, or to taste
½	cup water
1	tablespoon cornstarch

Christmas Joys

© SUCCESSFUL FARMING PUB. CO.

times with a fork, being careful to pierce the skin but not the meat. Loop the band of skin in the tail area over the ends of the legs to hold them together or, if the band is missing, leave the goose open, and set aside.

To make the stuffing: Tear the bread into 1-inch chunks and place them in a large bowl. Melt the butter in a medium skillet and sauté the onion and celery over medium heat until the onion is translucent, about 3 minutes. Add the sautéed vegetables, eggs, and broth to the bread chunks and season with salt and pepper to taste. Stir gently to mix well. Sprinkle on enough sage to cover the entire top of the mixture and stir again. Lightly grease a 3-quart casserole dish, add the stuffing, and set aside.

Cover the bottom of a roasting pan with water. Place the goose, breast side up, on a wire rack in the pan. Spray the goose lightly with cooking spray or rub it with a bit of butter or oil. Cover the roaster by crimping aluminum foil around the

edges and tenting the foil so it does not touch the goose breast. (If the goose's legs extend beyond the edge of your roaster, place a pan on the oven rack below the leg tips to catch any drippings.) Cook for 18 to 22 minutes per pound (4 to 5 hours) or until a meat thermometer placed deep into the thigh (without touching the bone) registers 180° to 185°F. Put the stuffing in the oven with the
continued

95

Best
Christmas
Wishes

To wish you a stocking
with presents stuffed high,
And plenty of plums in your Christmas pie.

Extension Circular 453   September 1949

Scandinavian Ideas
for a South Dakota
Christmas

EXTENSION SERVICE   SOUTH DAKOTA STATE COLLEGE
UNITED STATES DEPARTMENT OF AGRICULTURE COOPERATING

goose for the last hour of cooking time or, if you like crispy stuffing, the last 1½ hours. Transfer the goose to a serving platter. Let cool slightly before carving.

To make the sauce: Combine the plums, sugar, water, and cornstarch in a medium saucepan and cook over medium heat, stirring constantly, for about 5 minutes, or until the sauce thickens and clears. Serve over the sliced goose.

Serves 8 to 10

Variation: Put the stuffing in the goose, filling the neck and body cavities loosely. Loop the legs closed or leave the goose open. Roast for 25 to 30 minutes per pound, 5½ to 7 hours.

Note: For years, the Schiltz family has saved leftover goose for Grandma Schiltz's Goose Sandwiches. Refrigerate the drippings from the roasted goose. After the fat has coagulated, scrape it off and discard. Chop the leftover goose meat into chunks. Add the drippings and enough chicken broth to moisten and flavor the goose. Add finely diced onion and celery, and season to taste with salt, freshly ground pepper, and yellow or Dijon mustard, and mix. If you prefer a smoother sandwich filling, pulse the ingredients in a food processor.

Christmas Wishes

Holiday Bread Pudding

In 1866, Jack Daniel asked the government for a permit to make whiskey. Permission granted, he opened the country's first licensed distillery in Lynchburg and put Tennessee on the map as a maker of fine whiskey. Used as a flavoring for bread pudding, Tennessee whiskey elevates this traditional Southern brunch or dessert dish to celebratory party food. A bonus for the cook, as the whiskey evaporates during baking it fills the kitchen with a festive aroma. Serve warm, with a drizzle of heavy cream.

1	cup raisins
1	tablespoon fresh orange or lemon zest
⅓	cup Tennessee whiskey, preferably Jack Daniel's
7	cups cubed white bread (about 8 slices)
4	eggs
3	cups milk
1	cup sugar
1	teaspoon vanilla extract
4	tablespoons cold butter, cut into small pieces
	Freshly grated nutmeg
	Heavy whipping cream for drizzling

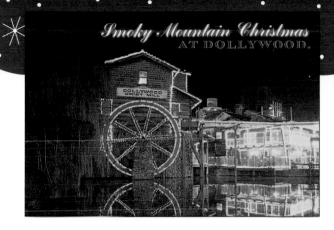

Combine the raisins, zest, and whiskey in a small bowl and let sit for 30 minutes, or until the raisins soften and get plump. Heat the oven to 400°F. Butter a 9-by-13-inch baking dish and set aside.

Arrange the bread cubes on a baking sheet and bake for about 5 minutes, or until lightly toasted. Transfer to the prepared pan. Combine the eggs, milk, sugar, and vanilla in a medium bowl and whisk until smooth. Sprinkle the soaked raisins and any liquid in the bowl evenly over the bread cubes. Pour the egg mixture evenly over the bread. Let the mixture sit for 30 minutes, to allow the bread to soften.

Lower the oven temperature to 375°F. Dot the pudding with butter and sprinkle with nutmeg to taste. Bake for 35 to 40 minutes, or until the top is golden brown and the center is set. Remove from the oven and let sit for 5 minutes. Run a knife all around the edges to keep the pudding from sticking to the pan as it cools. Serve warm, drizzled with heavy cream.

Note: Use any firm white, French, or sourdough bread, or a mixture of white and whole-wheat bread. Freeze slices of bread from the ends of loaves threatening to go stale until you have enough for the pudding. Let frozen slices thaw at room temperature for 30 minutes before cutting them into cubes.

Serves 10 to 12

Fabulous Fruitcake

Texans get into fruitcake in a big way. Since 1896, the Collin Street Bakery in Corsicana has sold its signature fruitcake, which contains pineapple and papaya, and lots and lots of pecans, but no liquor and no green things. The company says it makes at least 20,000 fruitcakes in a 90-day period and ships them to 196 countries. And some years back, Texas baker Gladys Farek Holub was inspired to use a cement mixer to create the world's largest fruitcake, which weighed 150 pounds and was shaped like the state of Texas. Her Lone Star treat earned her fame as a guest on *The Tonight Show* with Johnny Carson in 1990 and with David Letterman in 1991, along with a special exhibition at the Texas State History Museum in Austin. Her daughter has carried on the business, and you can buy one of those giant Texas fruitcakes from www.gladysfruitcakes.com. While both of these famous recipes remain a secret, the following Texas-style recipe rich in dried fruit and pecans has been developed to convert countless fruitcake haters.

$1^1/_4$	cups all-purpose flour
1	teaspoon baking powder
2	teaspoons ground ginger
$^1/_2$	teaspoon ground cloves
$^1/_2$	cup chopped dried pineapple
$^1/_2$	cup dried currants, raisins, or dried cranberries
1	cup chopped pecans
$^1/_2$	cup finely chopped candied ginger
1	teaspoon grated lemon zest
$^1/_2$	cup (1 stick) butter, softened
$^1/_3$	cup molasses
$^1/_3$	cup sugar
4	large eggs
1	teaspoon vanilla extract
$^1/_2$	cup apple cider
3 to 6	tablespoons Calvados (see Note)

A Merry Christmas And A Happy New Year
EL PASO, TEXAS

LULING, TEXAS

Heat the oven to 350°F. Grease an 8½-by-4½-by-2½-inch loaf pan, line the bottom and sides with waxed paper, and grease the paper. Trim any paper that hangs over the edges. Combine the flour, baking powder, ginger, and cloves in a medium bowl. Stir with a whisk to blend, and set aside. In another medium bowl, combine the fruit, pecans, candied ginger, and lemon zest. Set aside.

Cream the butter, molasses, and sugar in a mixing bowl using an electric mixer. Beat in the eggs, one at a time, along with the vanilla. Add one-third of the flour mixture to the butter mixture along with one-third of the cider, and repeat, beating for a total of 1 minute, until the batter is smooth. Stir in the fruit and nut mixture. Pour the batter into the prepared pan, smooth the top, and bake for 1 hour and 15 minutes, or until the top is golden and a toothpick inserted into the center comes out clean.

Let the cake cool in the pan for 10 minutes. Pour some of the Calvados over the top and let cool for another 10 minutes. Run a knife around the edges and gently unmold onto a rack. Let cool completely and store wrapped tightly in aluminum foil for up to 1 week. To store longer, pour the remaining 2 tablespoons of Calvados into a shallow bowl and soak an 18-inch length of cheesecloth. Lay a 24-inch length of plastic wrap out on the counter and cover it with the dampened cheesecloth. Place the cooled fruitcake on the cheesecloth and gently wrap it. Then wrap again with the plastic wrap and seal tightly. Unwrap fruitcake and sprinkle with several tablespoons of Calvados or sherry every 5 days for up to 1 month.

Serves 10 to 12

Note: A bottle of Calvados, a smooth apple brandy, often costs more than $20, but it is often available in the small "nips" size behind the counter at large liquor stores. One small bottle holds about 3 tablespoons.

Quick Peppermint-Stick Cake

Sometime during this holiday season you'll undoubtedly hear one of the Mormon Tabernacle Choir's Christmas CDs. Dating back to the 1850s, the choir is a venerable institution, and its Christmas concerts in Salt Lake City always draw a full house. In the spirit of using holiday time wisely, Mormon cook Julie Badger Jensen created this special Christmas dessert with a built-in shortcut: a store-bought cake as the base. It's a quick and easy recipe you can offer to friends and family with no apologies. Serve it on a large cake plate garnished with sprigs of fresh holly.

Put the peppermint sticks in a self-sealing plastic bag, seal, and crush with a mallet or rolling pin. Combine the cream and sugar in a mixing bowl and whip until stiff peaks form. Add the crushed candy and the food coloring, if using. Slice the cake horizontally into 3 layers using a sharp bread knife. Spread about one-fourth of the whipped cream mixture between each layer, stacking one layer on top of the other, and using the remaining mixture to cover the entire cake. Garnish the top and sides of the cake with the small candy canes.

2	peppermint sticks or candy canes
2	cups heavy whipping cream
2	tablespoons sugar, or to taste
2	drops red food coloring (optional)
1	large angel food cake
10	small candy canes

Chocolate Sauce

One	14-ounce can sweetened condensed milk
1	ounce unsweetened chocolate
1	tablespoon vanilla extract

Merry Christmas

To make the chocolate sauce: Combine the condensed milk and chocolate in a microwave-safe bowl and microwave on high for 2 minutes, or until the chocolate is melted. Add the vanilla and whisk until smooth. Let sit at room temperature for about 15 minutes, or until slightly cooled and thickened. Cut the cake into slices and pass around a pitcher of chocolate sauce.

Serves 8 to 10

A happy Xmas

Maple-Walnut Fudge

Vermont is famous for its maple trees and for its delicious syrup sold throughout the nation. Use Grade B, or cooking, syrup for this old-fashioned, grainy fudge with a delicious maple flavor. This recipe is adapted from a 1939 Rutland community cookbook. If you're making it ahead of time, hide it well. It tends to be wildly popular.

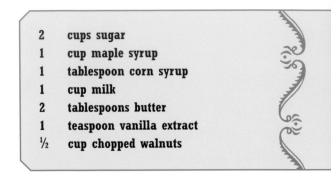

2	cups sugar
1	cup maple syrup
1	tablespoon corn syrup
1	cup milk
2	tablespoons butter
1	teaspoon vanilla extract
½	cup chopped walnuts

Lightly grease an 8-inch square baking pan. Combine the sugar, maple syrup, corn syrup, and milk in a large, heavy saucepan and stir until smooth. Clip a candy thermometer to the side of the pan and bring the mixture to a boil over medium-low heat. Without stirring, cook until the mixture reaches 236°F. Remove from the heat and add the butter, without stirring. Let the mixture cool to about 110°F. Add the vanilla, turn the mixture into a mixing bowl, and beat on low speed with an electric mixer just until the fudge loses its gloss. Add the nuts and immediately turn the mixture into the prepared pan, smoothing it with a spatula. Let cool for 10 minutes, then cut into squares. Let cool completely, then remove the

Christmas Greetings from Vermont

From dear old Vermont
A greeting shall hail you
With regards and good wishes
That never will fail you.

pieces from the pan. Store in an airtight container for up to 2 weeks.

Makes 12 to 16 pieces

VERMONT MAPLE SUGAR AND SYRUP

Including
DELICIOUS MAPLE RECIPES

VERMONT MAPLE SUGAR AND SYRUP

Including
DELICIOUS MAPLE RECIPES

Kodachrome
by
John Lovely

Williamsburg Wassail

Since 1936, Colonial Williamsburg has treated visitors to a charming and elegant Christmas celebration. It begins with the Grand Illumination, a spectacle of candles, fireworks, and music. There are concerts, special meals, and demonstrations of the village's signature craft: decorating with natural materials such as pine roping, evergreen boughs, and fresh fruit. And of course, no visit would be complete without a bit of holiday wassail. Based loosely on the old English drink for the New Year made with ale and apples, it's traditional for the master of the house in Williamsburg to wish visitors well with a hearty "Wass hael" ("Be well"). If you want to have hot wassail on hand during a party, follow the directions below and then pour it into a slow cooker set on high. After 30 minutes, reduce the temperature to low.

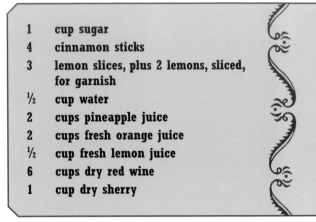

1	cup sugar
4	cinnamon sticks
3	lemon slices, plus 2 lemons, sliced, for garnish
½	cup water
2	cups pineapple juice
2	cups fresh orange juice
½	cup fresh lemon juice
6	cups dry red wine
1	cup dry sherry

Combine the sugar, cinnamon sticks, the 3 lemon slices, and the water in a stainless-steel pot. Bring to a boil and cook for 5 minutes. Strain the sugar syrup into a bowl and set aside. Discard the cinnamon sticks and lemon slices. Add the juices, wine, and sherry to the stockpot and bring to a simmer over medium heat. Do not boil. Add the sugar syrup and stir. Serve hot in mugs, garnished with lemon slices.

Serves 20

A Merry Christmas

Cast dull care away,
For here's to Xmas day.
Join the festive bowl,
And be a jolly soul.

Note: To make nonalcoholic wassail for 20 kids, combine 1 gallon apple cider, one 46-ounce can unsweetened pineapple juice, and ¾ cup herb or black tea in a stainless-steel pot. Tie 1 tablespoon whole cloves, 1 tablespoon allspice berries, and 2 broken cinnamon sticks in a square of cheesecloth and add to the pot. Bring to a low simmer over medium heat. Or, simmer in a slow cooker on low heat for 4 to 6 hours. Teach the kids to say "Wass hael," and you may well start a tradition.

Wassail! Wassail! All over the town
Our toast it is white and our ale it is brown
Our bowl it is made of the white maple tree
With the wassailing bowl, we'll drink to thee.

—*English wassail carol, from the 17th or 18th century*

Crunchy Christmas Slaw

With its rich soil, diverse climate, and large-scale irrigation, the Evergreen State produces abundant crops in every county. For more than 100 years, cranberries have been grown in the southwestern corner, many of them on 1,600 acres of peninsula land that sold for $1 an acre from 1872 to 1877. Here, they're combined with crunchy vegetables in a colorful salad that goes with any holiday fare.

Combine the cranberries, cabbage, celery, bell peppers, and grapes in a large bowl and stir gently until mixed.

To make the dressing: Combine all the ingredients in a small bowl and whisk until smooth. Pour about one-third of the dressing over the slaw, toss, cover tightly, and refrigerate until serving time. Reserve and refrigerate the remaining dressing. To serve, add the remaining dressing, toss well, and transfer to a glass bowl.

Serves 10 to 12 as a side dish

Variation: To save time, use packaged shredded cabbage.

½	cup chopped fresh cranberries
4	cups shredded green or napa cabbage
1	stalk celery, diced
1	green bell pepper, seeded and diced
1	red bell pepper, seeded and diced
1	cup red seedless grapes, halved
1	cup green seedless grapes, halved

Slaw Dressing

¼	cup apple juice
¼	cup mayonnaise
2	tablespoons honey
1	tablespoon apple cider vinegar

CHRISTMAS GREETING FROM WASHINGTON

WORLD LARGEST CHRISTMAS TREE
BELLINGHAM · WASH 1949
153 Ft High 4½ Ft ⌀ Base 145 years old photo by
10 Ft Cross at Top - 1000 Lights Ellis 2930

A Merry Christmas

A PATH
IN SCHMITZ PARK
SEATTLE
U.S.A

No. 616.

West Virginia

Hot Mulled Cider

Johnny Appleseed undoubtedly made his way through what today is West Virginia, and the state, which ranks ninth in U.S. apple production, is proud of its venerable orchards. The first Golden Delicious apple was developed in West Virginia in 1912 and was adopted as the official state fruit in 1995. Make this classic holiday drink with the freshest cider you can find. If you wish to add spirits, do so individually in each mug for the best flavor.

Combine the cider and sugar, if using, in a large stainless-steel pot. Lay a piece of cheesecloth about 8 inches square on the counter, put the spices in the center, bundle it up, and tie tightly with kitchen twine. Add the spice bag to the cider along with the lemon slices and bring almost to a boil over medium-high heat. Reduce the heat to low and simmer, partially covered, for about 1 hour. Remove the spice bag. Set out one mug for each guest. If using, add 2 tablespoons of spirits to each mug and top with hot cider. Sprinkle with nutmeg to taste and serve.

Serves 10 to 12

1	gallon apple cider
⅓	cup packed brown sugar (optional)
2	teaspoons whole cloves
2	teaspoons allspice berries
3	cinnamon sticks, each about 4 inches long
3	strips orange zest, each about 3 inches long
½	lemon, sliced
	Rum, brandy, or Calvados (optional)
	Freshly grated nutmeg

Variation: Top the cider with a spoonful of Spice Mixture (page 120).

CHRISTMAS JOYS.

All blessings on your Christmas hearth,
While greetings glad and gay
Ring out and mingle with the mirth
Of this most joyful day

H. M. Burnside.

A Happy Christmas.

Original only copyrighted

Copyrighted from present painting 1909 by The International Art Publishing Co. New York.

"Here's to a happy holiday,
Health and wealth for all the year."

Ellen H. Clapsaddle

111

Stollen

Early in the nineteenth century, German immigrants began to make their way to Wisconsin, and by 1860 they were in the majority in Milwaukee. Today, Christmas customs among the state's German American community include the baking and giving of stollen, which traditional bakers do not make with candied fruit. Baker and cookbook author Ken Haedrich developed this recipe using cottage cheese, an ingredient often used in Germany. Serve it as dessert on Christmas night, or enjoy it with coffee as a breakfast bread.

Combine the yeast and water in a small bowl. Stir to dissolve and let sit for about 5 minutes, or until foamy. Combine the cottage cheese, sugar, butter, and eggs in a food processor. Add the warm milk and purée. Pour the mixture into a large bowl. Stir in the vanilla, zest, salt, and yeast mixture. Add 3 cups of the flour and beat with a wooden spoon for 100 strokes. Cover the bowl with plastic wrap and set the sponge aside for 15 minutes.

2	packages active dry yeast
¼	cup warm (105°F to 155°F) water
¾	cup cottage cheese
¾	cup sugar
4	tablespoons unsalted butter at room temperature
2	eggs at room temperature
¾	cup milk, warmed
1	tablespoon vanilla extract
	Finely grated zest of 2 lemons or 2 oranges, or one of each
2	teaspoons salt
5 to 5½	cups unbleached all-purpose flour
1½	cups golden raisins
1½	cups dark raisins
1½	cups walnuts, toasted
4	tablespoons butter, melted
	Confectioners' sugar for dusting

Add enough of the remaining flour, about ½ cup at a time, to the sponge to make a soft, kneadable dough. Turn the dough out onto a floured surface and knead until smooth and elastic, about 8 minutes, using enough of the remaining flour to keep the dough from sticking. Place the dough in a lightly greased bowl and turn to coat the surface evenly. Cover the bowl with plastic wrap and set aside in a warm spot until doubled, 1½ to 2 hours. Combine the raisins and walnuts in a small bowl and set aside.

Turn the dough out on a floured work surface without punching it down. Roll the dough into a large rectangle about 1 inch thick. Spread the raisin mixture over the dough, gently pressing it in. Roll up the dough lengthwise. Cut the roll into 3 equal sections. Form each section loosely into a ball and place, seam side down, on the work surface. Cover loosely with plastic wrap and let rest for 10 minutes.

Roll each ball into an oblong strip about ½ inch thick. Fold each strip not quite in half lengthwise, so each one looks like a giant pair of lips, the upper one set back about 1 inch from the lower. Place one stollen on a lightly greased baking sheet and two on another, evenly spaced. Cover loosely with plastic wrap and set aside in a warm place until they begin to swell but before they double, 35 to 45 minutes.

Heat the oven to 350°F. Bake the stollen for 45 minutes; the surfaces will become quite dark. Transfer to a rack and immediately brush the tops and sides with melted butter. Let cool completely, then dust liberally with confectioners' sugar. Slip into self-sealing plastic bags.

Makes 3 loaves

Gingerbread Pancakes

Here's a way to enjoy the tantalizing taste of gingerbread for a holiday breakfast. Former ski instructors Ken and Sherrie Jern offer this hearty morning treat to guests who stay at their Wildflower Inn in Jackson Hole, where Christmas is a special time for the innkeepers and guests alike. Delicious with maple syrup, the pancakes also go nicely with yogurt, applesauce, or sliced pears. And they keep well in a warm oven, a plus for anyone who sleeps in.

Combine the flour, baking powder, salt, baking soda, cinnamon, and ginger in a large bowl (the batter will rise considerably) and stir with a whisk to blend. Combine the molasses and milk in another bowl. Beat in the eggs and melted butter. Add the wet ingredients to the dry ingredients and stir just until moistened.

2½	cups all-purpose flour
5	teaspoons baking powder
1½	teaspoons salt
1	teaspoon baking soda
1	teaspoon ground cinnamon
½	teaspoon ground ginger
¼	cup dark molasses
2	cups milk
2	eggs
6	tablespoons butter, melted
	Canola oil for greasing griddle

Heat a pancake griddle or heavy frying pan until a drop of water dances on the surface. Grease the griddle or pan, stir the dough down, and spoon about 2 tablespoons batter onto the griddle or pan, smoothing it out very gently to form each pancake about 4 or 5 inches across. When bubbles form evenly on the tops and the bottoms are lightly browned, about 1 minute, flip and cook until lightly browned on the other sides. Keep warm in a low oven. Repeat until all the batter is used. Serve hot, with butter and maple syrup.

Makes about sixteen 4-inch pancakes

Greetings from SANTA'S KITCHEN & REINDEER ROOM

Homemade gifts are always appreciated, and they make perfect presents for friends and neighbors. Pack any of these holiday treats in a colorful tin.

Glazed Curried Pecans

Use close-to-perfect pecan halves for this utterly addictive combination, which makes a great cocktail snack or dessert.

4	tablespoons butter, plus more for greasing
½	cup packed brown sugar
2	tablespoons milk
½	teaspoon curry powder
2	cups pecan halves
	Salt

Spread a sheet of aluminum foil about 24 inches long on the counter and grease it lightly with butter. Melt the 4 tablespoons butter in a large saucepan over medium-low heat. Add the brown sugar, milk, and curry powder and cook for 1 minute, stirring until smooth. Add the pecans and, using a rubber spatula, stir gently until they are evenly coated with the sugar mixture. Continue cooking for 10 minutes, stirring frequently, or until the pecans are coated with the glaze. Using the spatula, turn the pecans out onto the prepared foil and separate them. Sprinkle lightly with salt to taste and let cool for 30 minutes. Store in a tightly covered tin for up to 2 weeks.

Makes 2 cups

Peppermint Bark

Since you're not dealing with boiling hot syrup, this is a good recipe to make with kids. Let little helpers add the peppermint candies or help break the cooled candy into pieces.

1	pound white chocolate, chopped
⅔	cup crushed peppermint candies or candy canes
½	teaspoon peppermint extract

Line a baking sheet with aluminum foil. Melt the chocolate in a double boiler over barely simmering water, stirring frequently, until smooth. Remove from the heat and stir in the candies and peppermint extract. Pour the mixture into the prepared pan, letting it settle into an even layer, and let stand at room temperature for 2 hours, or refrigerate for 30 minutes, until firm. Lift the candy up with a spatula and break it into pieces. Store in a tightly covered tin for up to 4 weeks.

Makes about 1½ dozen pieces, depending on size

Chocolate Truffles

Use the very best ingredients you can buy to make these sinfully rich candies, since everything contributes to the ultimate taste. Use several kinds of coating to create an interesting assortment. Pack them in little tins and attach a note suggesting they be refrigerated for up to 4 weeks and set out for 30 minutes before serving.

1   **cup heavy whipping cream**
4   **tablespoons unsalted butter**
2   **tablespoons superfine sugar**
8   **ounces semisweet or bittersweet chocolate, finely chopped**
    Sifted unsweetened cocoa powder, finely chopped pecans, sifted confectioners' sugar, and/or finely chopped sweetened coconut

Combine the cream, butter, and sugar in a double boiler over barely simmering water, stirring several times until the butter melts. Remove from the heat, add the chocolate, and let sit for 1 minute. Stir until very smooth. Refrigerate for about 1 hour, or until the mixture is firm enough to shape. Set out one or several plates and arrange your choice of coatings, using about ¼ cup at a time. Set out a plastic container with a tight-fitting lid to hold the truffles. Remove the chilled mixture from the refrigerator and scoop out a teaspoonful. Using your hands, quickly but gently roll it into a ball, place it in one of the coatings, and continue

rolling on the coating plate to make an uneven ball. Place it in the container. Repeat until all the truffles are made, dusting your hands with confectioners' sugar to keep the chocolate from sticking if necessary and refrigerating the mixture again whenever it becomes too soft to handle. Put the cocoa-covered truffles in a sieve and shake gently to remove the excess cocoa. Refrigerate the finished truffles.

Makes 2 dozen

Variations: Add 2 to 3 tablespoons liqueur or Cognac.

Combine cocoa and confectioners' sugar in equal amounts as a coating.

Experiment with different chocolates, such as orange or espresso.

117

Gingerbread Cupcakes

These spicy treats, chock-full of zingy ginger, provide another take on gingerbread and are a nice change from a plate of cookies. Use holiday baking papers, and frost or sprinkle the cupcakes with confectioners' sugar.

¾   cup applesauce
½   cup dark molasses
1   teaspoon baking soda
1½   cups all-purpose flour
¼   teaspoon salt
2   teaspoons ground ginger
1   teaspoon ground cinnamon
½   teaspoon ground cloves
2   eggs
⅔   cup sugar
⅓   cup canola oil
½   cup finely chopped candied ginger

Cream Cheese Frosting

1   tablespoon cream cheese
1   tablespoon butter at room temperature
1   cup confectioners' sugar, sifted
     About 1 tablespoon milk

Heat the oven to 350°F. Line 12 muffin cups with baking papers. Combine the applesauce and molasses in a medium saucepan and cook over medium heat for about 1 minute, or until the mixture just begins to reach a boil. Stir in the

baking soda (the mixture will foam up) and remove from the heat. Set aside.

Combine the flour, salt, ginger, cinnamon, and cloves in a medium bowl and stir with a whisk to blend. Combine the eggs, sugar, and oil in a mixing bowl and beat with an electric mixer until smooth. With the mixer on low speed, add the flour mixture, beating just until the batter is smooth. Stir in the cooled molasses mixture and the candied ginger. Distribute the batter evenly among the muffin cups and bake for 20 minutes, or until the tops are firm and a toothpick inserted in the center comes out clean. Let the cupcakes cool in the pan for 10 minutes and then unmold them on a wire rack to finish cooling.

To make the frosting: Combine the cream cheese, butter, and sugar in a mixing bowl and beat until smooth. Add 1 tablespoon milk and beat well. Use a tiny bit more milk if necessary to reach a good spreading consistency. Spread the frosting on the cooled cupcakes. Store, tightly covered, for up to 1 week.

Makes 12

Tips for a Holiday Buffet

During the busy Christmas season, it's always fun to think about entertaining. But the reality of shopping, cooking, and serving food to a crowd can be downright overwhelming. Keep it simple by organizing a buffet supper for a stand-up meal, and follow this advice so you enjoy the party as much as your guests do.

Keep the menu simple. Include some of your favorite recipes. Make a big, colorful salad and slice up some fresh fruit. Never apologize for serving take-out or prepared foods along with dishes you make yourself. They can be great time-savers.

Get an early start. Do as much ahead of time as you can. Move the furniture, and set out the glasses, plates, napkins, and utensils. If possible, arrange the dining table so guests can reach it from all sides. Think about what will go where on the table, and use serving pieces such as cake stands and footed bowls to create visual interest. Make a list, shop, and do as much as you can the day before.

Don't reheat anything. Serve food that tastes best at room temperature so you never have to fuss about keeping things hot. Allow for a range of tastes among your guests, and set out a variety of foods they can mix and match: high-quality cold cuts, sliced cheeses, hearty breads, condiments, smoked salmon, raw vegetables, and tasty dips. Include some finger foods (deviled eggs, olives, nuts, grapes, one-bite appetizers) and napkins for guests who prefer to dart in and out.

Replenish platters. When serving shrimp or other expensive foods, don't put them all out at once. Bring out half or a third at a time and resupply as necessary so everyone gets a chance to eat some.

Downplay the sweets. Don't spend time making elaborate desserts, which can be hard to serve and eat at a buffet. Instead, set out a platter of homemade cookies and a bowl of Christmas candies.

Hire some help. You don't need caterers, but think about the kids in your neighborhood who would love to earn some Christmas money. Ask one or two to keep kitchen counters clear; patrol for dirty plates, glasses, and napkins; wash dishes; replenish platters of food; and take out the trash.

Dim the lights. Of course, the house will be immaculate before the party. But it never hurts to keep the light levels lower than usual to create a special atmosphere. Use lots of candles, ideally unscented ones, on the dining table, on side tables, at the front hall, in the kitchen. Dim overhead lights or turn them off altogether, and use table lamps for a softening effect.

Give a toast. Bring everyone together in a special way by telling a story or sharing some news, wishing everyone well, and thanking them for coming.

Serve this delightful hot drink as the grand finale at your buffet party. Multiply the recipe by the number of your guests.

1	teaspoon Spice Mixture (recipe follows)
2 to 3	tablespoons rum
2	tablespoons light cream or half-and-half
1	cup hot coffee
One	2-inch strip orange zest

Serves 1

Put the spice mixture into a coffee mug. Add the rum and cream. Pour in the hot coffee, stir until smooth, and garnish with the orange zest.

Spice Mixture

2	tablespoons butter
1	cup packed dark brown sugar
1	teaspoon ground cinnamon
½	teaspoon freshly grated nutmeg
¼	teaspoon ground allspice
¼	teaspoon ground cloves

Combine all ingredients in a food processor and pulse until evenly mixed and crumbly. Store in the refrigerator in a tightly sealed container. You will have 1½ cups, tightly packed, enough for 6 dozen coffees. Tightly covered, it will keep for weeks in the refrigerator.

Makes 1½ cups, enough for 72 servings

COFFEE 'ROUND the CHRISTMAS TREE

FESTIVE HOLIDAY RECIPES

Here are the recipes in this book, organized by category.

Christmas Recipes 1956

"The GAS Company"
CENTRAL ELECTRIC & GAS COMPANY

continued

Recipe Permissions

Arizona: Posole (page 16). From *Christmas in Arizona* by Lynn Nusom. Used by permission of Golden West Publishers (Phoenix, Arizona, 1992), www.goldenwestpublishers.com.

Arkansas: Nicholas Peay's Eggnog (page 18). Used by permission of Bill Worthen, Historic Arkansas Museum, Little Rock, www.arkansashistory.com.

California: Fuyu Persimmon and Radicchio Salad (page 20). Used by permission of Peggy Knickerbocker.

Colorado: Caramelized Lamb Roast with Apricot and Cranberry Stuffing (page 22). Used by permission of the American Lamb Board.

Connecticut: The Best-Ever Butter Cookies (page 24). Used by permission of Alice Lehr.

Delaware: Baked Ham with Madeira Sauce and Browned Potatoes (page 26). Used by permission of the Winterthur Museum and Country Estate.

Georgia: Cranberry-Pecan Chutney (page 30). Used by permission of the Georgia Pecan Commission.

Hawaii: Pineapple-Macadamia Nut Loaf Cake with Pineapple Sauce (page 32). Used by permission of Mike and Kim Crinella, www.alohafriendsluau.com.

Idaho: Baked Mashed Potatoes (page 34). Used by permission of the Idaho Potato Commission.

Illinois: Seafood Lasagna (page 36). Used by permission of Deborah Mele.

Indiana: Lebkuchen (page 38). Used by permission of the IUPUI Max Kade German American Center and Indiana German Heritage Society, www.serve.com/shea/germusa/lebkuch.htm.

Iowa: Corn Pudding (page 40). Used by permission of Bethia Waterman.

Kansas: Coffee Cake for a Crowd (page 42). Used by permission of the Kansas Wheat Commission, www.kswheat.com.

Kentucky: Chocolate Celebration Cake (page 44). Used by permission of Labrot & Graham.

Louisiana: Corn Bread Oyster Dressing (page 46). Used by permission of Carolyn Griffen.

Maine: Lobster Chowder (page 48). From *50 Chowders*, by Jasper White (Scribner: New York, 2002). Used by permission of Jasper White.

Maryland: Baked Christmas-Morning Oatmeal (page 52). Used by permission of John and Sallie Cwik, www.oldbrickinn.com.

Missouri: Oven-Roasted Chestnut Appetizers (page 62). Used by permission of the University of Missouri Center for Agroforestry, www.centerforagroforestry.org.

Montana: Venison Steaks au Poivre (page 64). Used by permission of Larry Copenhaver, *Montana Hunting and Fishing Journal*, www.huntingand-fishingjournal.org.

New Hampshire: Snowballs (page 70). Used by permission of Country Inns in the White Mountains, www.countryinnsinthe-white mountains.com.

New Jersey: Christmas Pea Salad (page 72). Used by permission of Doug and Anna McMain, The Queen Victoria B&B, www.queenvictoria.com.

New Mexico: Biscochitos (page 74). Used by permission of Nancy Gerlach, co-author with Dave DeWitt of *The Spicy Food Lover's Bible* (Stewart, Tabori & Chang: New York, 2005).

New York: Oyster Stew (page 76). Used by permission of Mary van der Ploeg Mallows.

North Dakota: Cranberry Scones (page 80). Used by permission of the North Dakota Wheat Commission.

Oklahoma: Aunt Bill's Brown Candy (page 84). Used by permission of Cynthia Townley Ewer.

Oregon: Cherry-Chocolate Torte (page 86). Used by permission of Oregon Fruit Products Co., www.oregonfruit.com.

Pennsylvania: Amish Christmas Caramel Corn (page 88). Used by permission of Margaret Schaut. From the Amish Christmas Web page, www.squidoo.com/amishchristmas.

Rhode Island: Tourtière (page 90). Used by permission Sue Gray and King Arthur Flour.

continued

South Dakota: Kathryn's Roast Goose Supreme with Sage Stuffing and Plum Sauce (page 94). Used by permission of Kathryn Schiltz.

Tennessee: Holiday Bread Pudding (page 98). Used by permission of Jack Daniel's Distillery, www.jackdaniels.com.

Utah: Quick Peppermint-Stick Cake (page 102). From *Essential Mormon Celebrations,* by Julie Badger Jensen (Deseret Book: Salt Lake City, 2005). Used by permission.

Virginia: Williamsburg Wassail (page 106). From *The Williamsburg Cookbook,* published by the Colonial Williamsburg Foundation. Used by permission. Wassail for Kids (page 106). Used by permission of Colonial Williamsburg, www.history.org.

Washington: Crunchy Christmas Slaw (page 108). Used by permission of the Washington State University Research Foundation.

Wisconsin: Stollen (page 112). Used by permission of Ken Haedrich.

Wyoming: Gingerbread Pancakes (page 114). Used by permission of Sherrie Jern, Wildflower Inn, www.jackson-holewildflower.com.

Illustration Credits

Cover: Postcard, 1914.

Front Flap: (from left) Embossed postcard, 1910; Postcard, ca. 1910.

1. Vintage DuPont family Christmas card, Winterthur Museum Archive.

2. (top) Embossed postcard, ca. 1910; (bottom) Christmas card, ca. 1950.

3. (top) Bavarian Festival parade float, chrome postcard, Frankenmuth, MI; (bottom) Christmas card, ca. 1950.

7. (clockwise from top left) Embossed postcard, 1914; Embossed postcard, 1904; Postcard, 1913; postcard, 1914.

8. (left) Postcard, ca. 1910; (right) Postcard, 1910.

9. Postcard, 1908.

10. Photograph by John Adams Davis, New York City, 1930.

11. Menu, Vinoy Park Hotel, St. Petersburg, FL, 1951.

12. Postcard, ca. 1920.

13. (left) Recipe book cover, © 1949 Church & Dwight; (right) page from California Walnut Growers Association cookbook, 1937.

14. Christmas card, © Spenglers, ca. 1960.

15. (top) Christmas card, © Spenglers, ca. 1960; (bottom) Souvenir envelope, ca. 1960.

16. Linen postcard, 1941.

17. Christmas cookbook cover, 1959.

18. Embossed postcard, ca. 1910.

19. Chrome postcard, Arkansas State Capitol, ca. 1950.

20. Embossed postcard, 1912.

21. (top) Postcard, ca. 1920; (bottom) Postcard, 1936.

23. Postcard folder, ca. 1965.

25. (clockwise from left) Embossed postcard, ca. 1910; Embossed postcard, ca. 1910; Jewelry catalog cover, © Hamilton Watch Company, 1954.

26. Die-cut trade card, Cudahy Packing Co., ca. 1900.

27. (top) Christmas card, ca. 1940; (bottom) Embossed postcard, ca. 1910.

29. (clockwise from left) Christmas card, ca. 1940; Linen postcard, 1937; Linen postcard, 1937; Real photo postcard, 1955.

30. Christmas store decorations catalog illustration, ca. 1950.

31. (clockwise from top left) Linen postcard, ca. 1935; Blotter, 1953; Linen postcard, Rich's Department Store, Atlanta, 1962.

32. Christmas store decorations catalogue illustration, ca. 1950.

33. (left) Embossed postcard, 1917; (right) Christmas Menu cover, Submarine Base, Pearl Harbor, Honolulu, HI, 1942.

35. (top) Postcard, 1915; (bottom) Postcard, 1919.

36. Menu cover, The Rock Island, 1901.

37. Postcard, 1911.

38. Linen postcard, 1942.

39. (from left) Chrome postcard, ca. 1950; Christmas postcard, 1950; Menu cover, © Santa Claus Land, 1951.

40. Postcard, 1919.

41. (top) Postcard, ca. 1910; (bottom) Postcard, 1911.

42. Pan American Coffee Bureau recipe booklet illustration, ca. 1970.

43. (top) Blotter, ca. 1920; (bottom) Postcard, ca. 1910; both from Hal Ottaway Collection.

44. (from left) Christmas store decorations catalogue illustration, ca. 1950; Embossed postcard, ca. 1910.

45. Chrome postcard, ca. 1950.

46. Christmas seals, 1933 and 1930.

47. (from left) Trade card, ca. 1900; Postcard, 1906.

48. (from left) Postcard, 1949; Christmas tree ornament, © by Christmas Club.

50. (top) Postcard, ca. 1915; (bottom) Postcard, 1943.

51. Hotel brochure and brochure illustration, ca. 1940s.

52. Embossed postcard, 1910.

53. Chrome postcard, ca. 1950.

54. Postcard, ca. 1920.

55. Christmas catalog, 1906.

56. Postcard, 1913.

57. (clockwise from top) Chrome postcard, ca. 1950; Embossed postcard, 1910; Postcard, ca. 1910.

58. Christmas card, ca. 1950.

59. Dinner and dance invitation, 1877, Joanne Cassullo Collection.

60. Christmas card, ca. 1940s.

61. (from left) Menu, 1943; Recipe card, ca. 1970s.

continued

visit **BRONNERS of FRANKENMUTH, MICH.**
SEE AMERICA'S LARGEST YEAR 'ROUND DISPLAY OF CHRISTMAS DECORATIONS

Index

Table of Equivalents

The exact equivalents in the following table have been rounded for convenience.

Liquid/Dry Measures

U.S.	METRIC
¼ teaspoon	1.25 milliliters
½ teaspoon	2.5 milliliters
1 teaspoon	5 milliliters
1 tablespoon (3 teaspoons)	15 milliliters
1 fluid ounce (2 tablespoons)	30 milliliters
¼ cup	60 milliliters
⅓ cup	80 milliliters
½ cup	120 milliliters
1 cup	240 milliliters
1 pint (2 cups)	480 milliliters
1 quart (4 cups; 32 ounces)	960 milliliters
1 gallon (4 quarts)	3.84 liters
1 ounce (by weight)	28 grams
1 pound	448 grams
2.2 pounds	1 kilogram

Lengths

U.S.	METRIC
⅛ inch	3 millimeters
¼ inch	6 millimeters
½ inch	12 millimeters
1 inch	2.5 centimeters

Oven Temperatures

FAHRENHEIT	CELSIUS	GAS
250	120	½
275	140	1
300	150	2
325	160	3
350	180	4
375	190	5
400	200	6
425	220	7
450	230	8
475	240	9
500	260	10